The Open University

A220 Princes and Peoples: France and the British Isles, 1620–1714

Block 2: Society and culture 1620-1714

First published in 1994 by

The Open University

Walton Hall

Milton Keynes

United Kingdom

MK7 6AA

Reprinted 1996, 1999

ISBN 0 7492 8549 4

Edited, designed and typeset by The Open University.

This book is a component of the Open University course A220 *Princes and Peoples: France and the British Isles, 1620–1714*. Details of this and other Open University courses are available from the Central Enquiry Service, The Open University, PO Box 200, Walton Hall, Milton Keynes, MK7 6YZ, tel.: 01908 653078.

Printed and bound in Great Britain by Bell and Bain Ltd, Glasgow

2.1

21276C/a220b2pli2.1

Contents

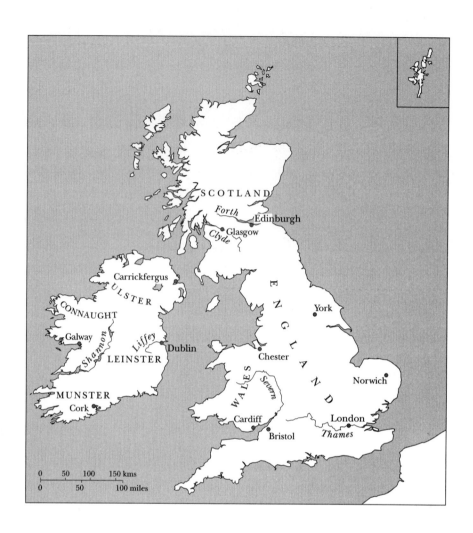

SCOTLAND

Forth
Edinburgh
Clyde Glasgow

Carrickfergus

ULSTER

CONNAUGHT

ENGLAND

York

Galway

Shannon Liffey Dublin

LEINSTER

Chester

WALES

Severn

Norwich

MUNSTER

Cardiff

London

Cork

Bristol Thames

| 0 | 50 | 100 | 150 kms |
| 0 | | 50 | 100 miles |

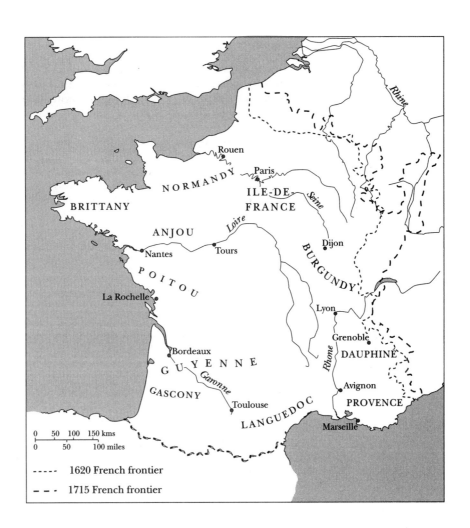

Rouen

Paris

ILE-DE-FRANCE

NORMANDY

Seine

BRITTANY

ANJOU

Loire

Dijon

BURGUNDY

Nantes

Tours

POITOU

La Rochelle

Lyon

Grenoble

Rhône

DAUPHINÉ

Bordeaux

GUYENNE

Garonne

GASCONY

Avignon

PROVENCE

Toulouse

LANGUEDOC

Marseille

Rhône

| 0 | 50 | 100 | 150 kms |
| 0 | | 50 | 100 miles |

----- 1620 French frontier

- - - 1715 French frontier

Introduction

The previous block was about the upheavals which split France and the different parts of the British Isles in the 1640s and 1650s. This block is concerned with the social, religious and administrative changes which took place in the societies of those countries throughout the period 1620–1714. Some of these changes were the result of the upheavals of the 1640s and 1650s, some contributed to them and some seem to have simply coincided with them without there being any obvious connection. As you work through the units you may wish to think about the extent to which longer-term social, religious and administrative changes were caused by, or themselves contributed to causing, the upheavals.

Unit 6
Education, literacy and propaganda

Prepared for the course team
by Lucille Kekewich

Contents

Study timetable

Weeks of Study	Texts	Video	AC	Set books
2	Unit 6; *Anthology*, II. 1–6; Offprint 11	6	AC1, section 3	Coward, Briggs

Objectives

By the end of this unit you should be able to:

1   appreciate how church and state intervened in education in France and the British Isles;

2   understand the problems in making accurate estimates of levels of literacy, but recognize that the general tendency was for them to rise;

3   recognize the political and social importance of 'salons', academies and learned societies;

4   appreciate how audiences for the written word were created and the variety of the products of the presses;

5   appreciate the impact of propaganda and of censorship on religion and politics.

The main themes of this unit are the ways in which various kinds of cultural influences could shape popular and élite ideologies and the role of the states and their established churches in promoting or opposing those influences.

Education and the state

What opportunities existed within the British Isles and France for the acquisition of a formal education? Many people learnt to read and some learnt to write without recourse to a recognized teacher and without attending a school. They are important in any history of literacy, but less interesting for the purposes of this unit, where the presence or absence of state intervention is a major concern.

Exercise Read Briggs, pp.173–4, 189 and Coward, pp.66–71. What kinds of control would you expect to find exercised over education in France and the British Isles

Discussion The two main sources of control over education were the respective churches and states. The problem in answering this question is to disentangle what precisely were their roles. Apart from brief periods during the Frondes, the French monarchy exercised effective control over the state throughout our period. The kings and the great majority of their subjects were orthodox members of the Catholic church and the formal education received by children reflected this fact. Excluded from this cosy arrangement were the Huguenots who could only provide for their own schooling in strictly designated areas, and the Jansenists who were periodically persecuted, accused of holding unorthodox beliefs.

The situation was even more complicated in the British Isles. In England and Wales Stuart monarchs attempted to enforce conformity to the Anglican church although, after 1689, dissenters were tolerated. During the Interregnum such control as there was tended to be exercised by the Presbyterians and the Independents who controlled the remains of the established church. The Presbyterian Church of Scotland provided a reasonable standard of schooling in the Lowland areas, in the Highlands education was a rare experience. This also applied to rural Ireland where the minority Anglican Church of Ireland and the English administration sought the conversion of Catholics but in a somewhat half-hearted fashion.

In practical terms, when the authority of the state and of the established churches was strong in France and the British Isles, some degree of control over education could be exercised by both. The state regularly punished those who did not conform to officially sanctioned beliefs and could exercise censorship over their literature. The churches actually provided many of the schools and teachers in both states and could persecute deviants through the use of the Papal Index of forbidden books in France and by hauling them before the church courts in England.

Figure 1
The Godly Minister,
woodcut from
Penny Godliness,
Pepys Library, 10, 194.
Reproduced by permission of
the Master and Fellows,
Magdalen College,
Cambridge.

It was amongst the common people, at the elementary stage, that church control over education could be at its weakest. Many members of the clergy in France and the British Isles included teaching amongst their duties. Yet the church hierarchies could exercise little supervision over

the content of their curricula and some of the clergy were, in any case, only partially educated themselves. In Britain numbers of clergy held Calvinistic beliefs and this was bound to be reflected in their teaching. In many areas the local school-teacher was a lay person, who had to conform to the orthodoxy of the established church. Yet their own intellectual capacities were often limited and the opportunities enjoyed by church or state to exercise any effective control were frequently minimal. The fervent Jansenist bishop of Alet for example found, during a tour of his diocese in the Pyrenees, villages where the services and the teachings of the church were practically unknown (Schimmelpenninck, 1813, p.41).

The reminiscences of Thomas Tryon, a young shepherd in Oxfordshire in the 1640s, indicate the casual, unsupervised way in which the poor could acquire an elementary education:

> ... in a little time having learnt to read competently well, I was desirous to learn to write, but was at a great loss for a master, none of my fellow shepherds being able to teach me. At last, I bethought myself of a lame young man who taught some poor peoples' children to read and write; and having by this time got some two sheep of my own, I applied myself to him, and agreed to give him one of my sheep to teach me to make the letters and join them together. (Spufford, 1981, p.29)

At elementary level educational opportunities were better for boys than for girls and, since attendance usually had to be paid for, fewer families were inclined to send their daughters to school. French girls were probably better placed than their British counterparts. A number of convents offered schooling of varying quality to girls up to the age of about eighteen. The Ursulines, an order founded during the Catholic Reformation, had 320 convents throughout France by the end of the seventeenth century. In England girls as well as boys might benefit from charitable foundations; in the 1670s, for example, Sir Harwood William Turner founded a school for 10 boys and 10 girls at Kirkleatham, Cleveland.

The most spectacular advance in female education in France was in 1684 when Louis XIV, at the instance of Madame de Maintenon, founded the school of St Cyr (three miles from Versailles) for 250 needy girls of noble birth. The teachers were celibate but their rule was not as rigorous as were those for most contemporary orders of women. Lougée (1976) sees this as the policy of a group of pious, aristocratic reformers who pinned their hopes on the eldest son of the Dauphin. She suggests that evidence of links between Fénelon (see Block 3, Unit 13) and Maintenon was deliberately suppressed after his disgrace.

Exercise   Read *Anthology*, II.1A. What were the principal objectives of the regulations?

Discussion   Through imposing a mode of behaviour which was modest and restrained, Madame de Maintenon and Louis XIV hoped to produce young women who would be obedient daughters of the church, good subjects and docile wives. The prohibition on reading books which had not been provided by the school establishes the narrow context in which St Cyr operated. The requirement to wear a uniform mode of dress, however, was probably to safeguard the sensibilities of the poorest pupils in an age when considerable prestige was attached to finery. Rule 8 looks like an encouragement to the girls to decide whether they had a vocation for the conventual life or wished to marry. Rules 9 and 10 asserted the power of the king and of Madame de Maintenon, who had formulated the regulations, to dominate every aspect of the pupils' lives.

In her letters Madame de Maintenon regretted some of the results of her educational system. She condemned traits (which nowadays would perhaps be regarded as positive qualities) in the girls, they were 'disputatious … inquisitive, bold'. It is clear from her Rules that she wished to produce intellectually bland, submissive pupils. She was anxious to preserve her school from the slightest danger of scandal, the excellent plays she had commissioned must not be performed before men.

The education available to older French boys was of variable quality and could only be enjoyed by a small section of the population. The Jesuits ran some good schools where the curriculum concentrated on grammar and religion, whilst that of the Oratorians was gradually broadening to include subjects such as the natural sciences. In England the Anglican hierarchy recognized the importance of establishing and maintaining schools which would prepare boys for the universities, the traditional route taken by those who wished to be ordained as clergymen.

Exercise Consult Coward, pp.67–9. What opportunities were available for English boys to obtain a good secondary education?

Discussion Two statistics quoted by Coward are impressive: the foundation of 142 grammar schools in the first half of the century and the fact that the number of graduate teachers in London more than doubled between the 1580s and 1630s. (Incidentally, did you think to consult footnote 107 to see what sources this information was based on?) The prospects were good for the boys who managed to get places at grammar schools, but they only catered for a small proportion of the male population. There were other ways of entering the professions, for example, training in the law could be acquired at the Inns of Court in London, and many prosperous families employed tutors to educate their children.

In Scotland in 1616 two Acts of Parliament were passed which expressed the anxiety of the state. The first Act provided for the establishment of a school and schoolmaster in every parish at the parishioners' expense. It also attacked Gaelic and sought to enforce the use of English so that the 'irish language which is one of the chief, principal causes of the continuance of barbarity and incivility in the Highlands may be abolished and removed'. The second Act ordered the compulsory education of the children from the clans in Lowland schools. No one was allowed to inherit property unless he was literate and well versed in spoken English (O'Day, 1982, p.227).

Exercise   What was the legislation for Scotland described above attempting to achieve?

Discussion The Protestant, Lowland Scots were launching an attack on the fabric of Highland society through their education policy. Many Highlanders were still Catholic and the Gaelic language emphasized their separation from Lowland Scotland and from England and the autonomy they tried to preserve for their clans. (Some chieftains were Protestant, by this time, and they colluded with parliament.) The establishment of parish schools throughout Scotland represented a determined effort to enlighten and 'Protestantize' the common people and to encourage them to conform to the kind of religion the General Assembly in Edinburgh wished to propagate.

These measures were only partially effective: O'Day (1982, p.228) remarks, for example, that by 1650 in Aberdeenshire, only 28 out of 83 parishes had schools. Yet the Presbyterian Church of Scotland, before and after the Act of Union of 1707, certainly encouraged the spread of education. Scotland had more universities and a higher proportion of university educated men than did England.

   In Ireland many Catholic priests taught the rudiments of religion to the children in their flocks, but there were few other educational opportunities available to the poor. Richer Catholics could send their children abroad to monasteries, convents and universities. Canny (1982, pp.91–116) believes that during settled times priests tended to encourage a knowledge of English, as well as the native Gaelic. They felt that it was a practical necessity to be able to communicate with the conquerors in their own language. Conversely, the Anglican Church of Ireland saw no need to encourage its ministers to learn Irish. The ascendant Anglicans had schools within the Pale and Trinity College, Dublin was their university. This institution was in decline by the middle of the century and some educationalists under Cromwell attempted to reform it and make it the centre of a scheme for secondary and higher education in Ireland. Little came of these plans but they show the importance the Protectorate attached to education as a means of civilizing the most troublesome of the British Isles. Similar motives informed a project to found a Welsh college, but it too came to nothing (O'Day, 1982, p.266).

Exercise   Basing your answer on your reading from Coward and Briggs, and the material on Scotland, Ireland and Wales, estimate the extent to which the churches and the state directed education within the British Isles and France.

Discussion In France, at the elementary level, geographical factors were important: in remote parts the education of the poor depended on the abilities and energy of the local priests and bishops. This was also true, to some extent, of the influence exercised by the Anglican church in England. The Church of Scotland managed to provide a reasonable standard of elementary schooling in the Lowlands, and tried through education to bring the Highlanders to heel. In Ireland, beyond the Pale, the English government never made a serious effort to offer an education to the poor.

Middle- and upper-class men who were members of the established churches in France and the British Isles had a reasonable choice of opportunities at all stages of education. The churches dominated the universities and the legal professions had their own systems for inducting young lawyers. Only those who dissented from the established church encountered serious problems. Huguenots, up to the revocation of the Edict of Nantes, probably fared better in France than did the Catholics in Britain, although their rights were gradually eroded. In both countries the state sought to bar those who would not conform to the orthodox religion from the universities. The intervention of educational reformers during the Interregnum in England established a relatively liberal tradition in higher education which survived the Restoration. In France the great urban educational institutions, the universities and the Jesuit and Oratorian colleges reflected the authoritarian tendency of post-Tridentine Catholicism.

We shall now look at some school buildings as an additional source of information. So, now turn to Video 6.

Interpreting schools

 Few school buildings survive in an intact enough state to allow us to generalize about pedagogy or literacy. But by asking the right questions we can learn other things. They can show us how religious beliefs influenced educational benefactions and how schooling acted as an agency of social control.

Looking at the three examples of schools (see Illustration Book, Pls 33–37), we shall concentrate upon the following questions:

1   Who were the patrons (lay or clerical, an individual or a group)?

2   How was the foundation endowed and how much did it cost?

3   Why was this site and location chosen?

4   How was it governed and who regulated the teacher?

5   How was the school organized? We need to take into account the plan of the buildings, the arrangement of the classrooms, whether there was a chapel, how many people taught, whether there was accommodation for the teacher(s), who was taught and how they were selected, and what the curriculum was.

6   How does the architecture, decoration and symbolism relate to the contemporary ideas about authority, politics and religion?

Video Exercise 1   Now watch Part 1 of Video 6 (Heriot's Hospital) making notes on the six questions.

Discussion   We can't answer all of the questions fully for lack of evidence, but these are some of the points you should have noted.

    The symbolic role of the founder, a successful Scottish merchant who had vastly increased his fortune by following the king to London. By hard work and godliness he had prospered and was able to advertise his good fortune by a conspicuous act of public charity.

    This was plainly conceived of as a charitable foundation, its name 'hospital' (place of refuge) indicates that.

    The use of sculpture: symbols and emblems, cupids and swags is associated with the grandest kind of building, royal palaces. The king's master mason was using his talents in a display of civic pride. Yet these profane decorations are moderated by the Christian allusions and the admonitory mottoes.

    The school was a Presbyterian foundation and its government, curriculum and religious observances would have reflected that. Balcanquall, though not himself Presbyterian, was using religion as a means of promoting authority, obedience and piety. The building contains a curious mixture of court style and Christian allusion.

    It was plainly a successful foundation. Well planned, well endowed and well built, its dominating position could be a source of pride to the governors who executed the building and ran the foundation.

Video Exercise 2   Corsham free school was founded with the almshouses (which you have seen in TV7 and which we shall look at in detail in Video 9) by Lady Margaret Hungerford, childless widow of Sir Edward Hungerford, a prominent Wiltshire parliamentarian who had died in 1648. Although a Puritan, she conformed to the established church in 1660.

    The charity was controlled by the schoolmaster. The endowment provided for him generously, as generously as many ecclesiastical livings of the period. He had a house, brewhouse, kitchen, stables, orchard and gardens and £20 a year for his 'encouragement and maintenance'. His obligations were to administer the charity, supervise the almshouses, hold two services a day, and teach ten poor boys.

    Now watch Part 2 of the video making notes on the six questions.

Discussion   You shouldn't have much difficulty with the questions, though we don't know how much the school cost.

    To what degree is the school a Puritan school? Lady Hungerford may have been a Puritan, but she was also a gentlewoman who had conformed to the established church. By founding her charity she was establishing the authority of her status and of her view of the practice of religion through the schoolmaster's control of inmates and boys.

    The English gentry maintained social control by means of the parish church (we shall see something of this in Video 7). Lady Hungerford also maintained it by her patronage of the schoolmaster and the obedience of pupils and almspeople.

Was it a successful school? It was a medieval custom to combine school and almshouse in one foundation, but was already old-fashioned by the seventeenth century. Here it meant that the schoolmaster could not devote himself to teaching alone and the fixed number of pupils offered little incentive to him to improve the school to attract more pupils.

Video Exercise 3   Appleby Magna school was founded by Sir John Moore, second son of the owner of the manor. He was born nearby in 1620 but left for London and made a fortune as a lead merchant and by investing in the East India and Guinea trades. Originally Nonconformist, he conformed to the established church in 1660, and was knighted in 1672. He was Lord Mayor of London in 1681–2. He had no male heirs and as he grew older he supported a number of London charities. In about 1690 he decided to found a free school in Appleby Magna for the boys of Appleby and the neighbouring villages. Two of his nephews lived in the area and acted as his agents while Sir John, who never left London or saw the school, directed operations by letter. His demands were exacting, it was *his* school. Some of the bills and correspondence survive and allow us to trace its evolution in detail.

Sir John had supplied the lead for the rebuilding of St Paul's cathedral where he must have met Sir Christopher Wren. Wren supplied elevations and plans for the school building which was to provide teaching space for the boys and accommodation for two masters. Wren also proposed that the school should take fee-paying boarders who could be accommodated above the hall. This, he argued, would remove the inconvenience of boys boarding in the village and keep then under the eye of the masters. It would also provide them with a financial incentive to run a good school and allow the foundation to pay lower wages.

The ornament and local execution of the project was entrusted to the local architect and sculptor, Sir William Wilson, who adapted Wren's design (he claimed later that this was with Wren's approval). Two of Wilson's ideas were sensible and functional. The flat roof provided more room for the dormitories on the top floor and the covered arcade provided a space for the boys to play in bad weather. Wilson also supplied a cupola in place of Wren's bell tower. A gallery was provided in the parish church at a cost of £10 for the pupils to attend services there. The school was opened in 1697.

The building cost £2,800, though the cost of the site and other expenses brought the total to about £4,000. Sir John expected to get materials and labour at favourable rates and to draw on the assistance of the local gentry for transport. Wilson tried to charge £250, but eventually received £126, while Wren provided his services free.

The school was governed by trustees, including members of the Moore family, and the local gentry and the early masters appear to have run the school responsibly.

Now watch Part 3 of the video making notes on the six questions. Your answers will help you with video exercise 4.

Video Exercise 4   What general similarities and differences can we see between these schools? Can we draw any wider conclusions?

Discussion The schools were alike in that all were for boys. They were all founded by lay patrons with London connections. This was probably because of London's importance as a centre for mercantile wealth rather than the influence of metropolitan culture which seems only to have been evident in the case of Sir John Moore's school.

The schools perpetuate the memories of their founders in different ways. Heriot's preserved his memory in the form of an exemplary act of charity after his death. He is represented as a historical figure in his everyday Jacobean clothes, symbolically supervising the life of the school. Sir John Moore is attired in contemporary dress, perhaps less as a symbol than as a role model, a latter-day Dick Whittington. Lady Hungerford perpetuates the memory of her family and connections in her coats of arms rather than her own person.

Heriot's Hospital has a proper chapel; Corsham school has a schoolroom which was used for services, but the boys of Sir John Moore's school had to attend the parish church. We can't necessarily deduce that the curriculum there was less religious, but there may have been an attempt to separate the sacred and the secular.

The schools offered their pupils different kinds of educational opportunities, whilst probably fulfilling their aims equally well. There are enough differences between them for us to be able to say that there is no such thing as a typical school of the period.

The literacy question

How should literacy be defined in the context of seventeenth-century society? It is all very well for the *Shorter Oxford Dictionary* to equate literacy with the ability to read and write, but is this satisfactory for a period when up to 90 per cent of the population in some areas could do neither? We may suppose that many people were motivated to learn to read so that they could have personal access to the Bible, but they had no such reason to acquire the skill of writing. How much ability did people have to possess to be defined as 'able to write'? Should they simply be capable of signing their name, doing joined-up writing, copying from a book or composing their own sentences?

In practice, we must adopt the working definition of literacy generally accepted by writers on the subject in France and the British Isles, which is determined by the nature of the surviving evidence. Any method of deciding on the extent of literacy at a particular time and place must rely on a sufficiently large sample to be useful. Signatures on legal documents, marriage contracts, petitions, religious agreements etc. survive in large numbers from the seventeenth century. Sometimes the signature is

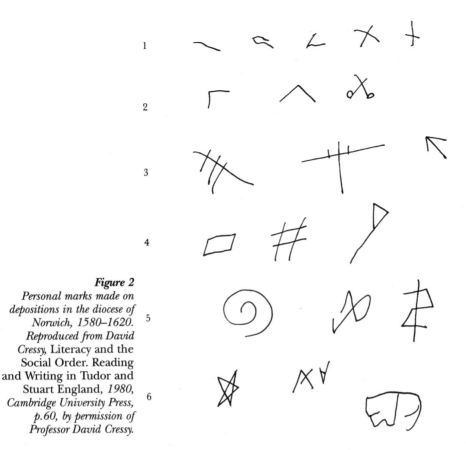

Figure 2
*Personal marks made on
depositions in the diocese of
Norwich, 1580–1620.
Reproduced from David
Cressy,* Literacy and the
Social Order. Reading
and Writing in Tudor and
Stuart England, *1980,
Cambridge University Press,
p.60, by permission of
Professor David Cressy.*

Row 1: simple scrawls and crosses; 2: mason, husbandman, tailor; 3: thatcher, woolcomber, fletcher; 4: brickmaker, brickmaker, baker; 5: tailor, glazier, worsted weaver; 6: mason, merchant, yeoman.

accompanied by information about the status and profession or work of the signatory and in many cases the date and location of the document is known.

Historians encounter difficulties in trying to estimate levels of literacy. The evidence is very uneven; the records are diverse; and ability to sign one's name is not necessarily evidence of the capacity to read and write. Some people could write their names without being literate and sometimes professional scribes signed on people's behalf. Conversely, those who could read and write sometimes chose to make a mark (as most illiterate people did) rather than signing, because they were very old or ill. However, historians have done a good deal of work on levels of literacy and have produced some statistics as a gauge of the effectiveness of seventeenth-century education. Levels of literacy affected the extent to which the population could engage with religious and political debates and thus can help us to understand some of the reasons for the crises and conflicts of the period.

Exercise Look at Tables 1, 2 and 3 (read the headings carefully as well as the statistics) and Figures 3 and 4 and give an opinion on their strengths and weaknesses as indicators of literacy levels.

Table 1   Percentages of literacy in some French towns, from parish registers of marriages

Town	Date	Percentage of male signatures	Percentage of female signatures
Reims (Marne)	1668–1699	65	42
Honfleur (Seine-Maritime)	1690–1699	57	28
Angers (Maine et Loire)	1697–1698	53	43
Rennes (Ille et Vilaine)	1697–1698	46	32
Rouen (Seine-Maritime)	1697–1698	57	38
Aix-en-Provence (Bouches du Rhone)	End of 17th century	34	13

This information was collected by Louis Maggiolo, 1877–80. He was employed by the French government to review the extent of literacy from the late seventeenth century to his own time. His statistics were based on the reports of schoolmasters and mistresses throughout France.

Source: Chartier, Compère and Julia (1976, p.93).

Table 2   Occupational illiteracy of Scottish and Northern English male deponents (participants in legal cases), 1640–99 and 1700–70

	England		Scotland	
	1640–99	1700–70	1640–99	1700–70
Professional	(80) 3	(103) 0	(238) 3	(377) 1
Gentry/Laird	(211) 0	(74) 0	(132) 1	(188) 3
Craft & Trade	(551) 43	(673) 26	(248) 25	(938) 18
Yeoman/Tenant	(287) 49	(300) 26	(31) 26	(201) 32
Husbandman	(110) 75	(83) 42	Not applicable	
Labourer	(196) 85	(148) 64	(22) 82	(73) 68
Servant	(62) 73	(86) 50	(121) 58	(397) 55
Soldier	(51) 55	(35) 46	(40) 65	(121) 39
Unknown	(863) 62	(225) 30	(540) 51	(1,149) 47
Total	(2,411)	(1,727)	(1,372)	(3,489)

The figures in round brackets are numbers sampled, those unbracketed are percentages illiterate.

Source: Houston (1985, p.33). Reproduced by permission of Dr R.A. Houston.

Figure 3
Illiteracy in England, 1641–4: percentages of men unable to sign their names(bracketed percentages are based on fewer than 500 subscribers). Reproduced from David Cressy, Literacy and the Social Order. Reading and Writing in Tudor and Stuart England, *1980, Cambridge University Press, p.74 by permission of Professor David Cressy.*

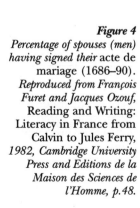

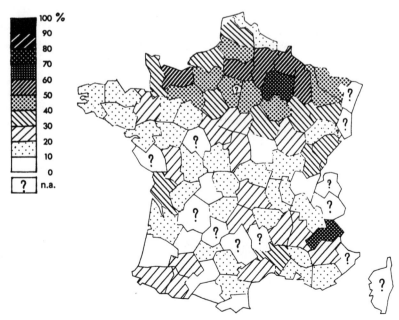

Figure 4
Percentage of spouses (men) having signed their acte de mariage *(1686–90). Reproduced from François Furet and Jacques Ozouf,* Reading and Writing: Literacy in France from Calvin to Jules Ferry, *1982, Cambridge University Press and Editions de la Maison des Sciences de l'Homme, p.48.*

Table 3   Male Illiteracy in England, 1641–4 (subscribers to the Protestation, Vow and Covenant and the Solemn League and Covenant)

County	Usable parishes	No. of subscribers	No. mark[1]	% mark
Berkshire	12	725	535	74
Buckinghamshire	3	156	110	71
Chester city	5	736	385	52
Cornwall	116	15,868	11,426	72
Derbyshire	3	316	235	74
Devon	38	4,903	3,527	72
Dorset	9	573	400	70
Durham	2	247	183	74
Essex	16	1,081	681	63
Hertfordshire	1	85	63	74
Huntingdonshire	28	1,933	1,299	67
Lincolnshire	48	3,152	2,304	73
London	4	609	132	22
Middlesex	3	392	242	62
Norfolk	4	146	105	72
Nottinghamshire	49	3,845	2,930	76
Oxfordshire	4	288	190	66
Shropshire	1	67	44	66
Somerset	4	904	577	64
Staffordshire	3	312	201	64
Suffolk	6	294	131	45
Surrey	18	1,228	837	68
Sussex	28	1,797	1,272	71
Westmorland	7	797	591	74
Yorkshire	2	639	475	74
Total	414	41,093	28,875	70

[1] 'No. mark' = number of persons making a mark (unable to sign their names).

Source: Cressy (1980, p.73). Reproduced by permission of Professor David Cressy.

Discussion   We are not, of course, comparing like with like. Table 1 only gives the figures for signatures in parish registers of young married people during the last decade of the seventeenth century in six French towns and cities. The map of France (Fig. 4) showing levels of male literacy only covers four years, 1686–90. The numbers on which the percentages are based are not provided: note, incidentally, that the table and map count those who were *literate*, all the English and Scottish tables gauge levels of *illiteracy*. Table 2 gives the figures for male deponents (participants in legal cases) in England and Scotland, 1640–99 and 1700–70. Table 3 gives the numbers of English male subscribers to the Protestation, Vow and Covenant and the Solemn League and Covenant, 1641–4. The map of England gives a visual account of the information contained in Table 3. The numbers involved in Tables 2 and 3 are quite large, so they probably give a good indication of literacy levels. Table 2 breaks down the deponents according to their occupation and this is very enlightening. Since the upper categories enjoyed higher levels of literacy, we might suspect that, in Tables 1 and 3, in the places where literacy was relatively common, Reims and London for example, more members of the upper categories of society were signatories, but this can only be surmised. You could draw a number of such conclusions from these tables but they always should be prefaced by a cautious 'perhaps' or 'probably'.

Exercise   Look at the column of female signatories in Table 1 and at Tables 4 and 5. What comparison may be drawn between the levels of literacy amongst women in England, France and Scotland?

Table 4   Female illiteracy in London and East Anglia, 1580–1730

Decade		Norfolk/Suffolk			London/Middlesex	
	No.	No. mark	% mark	No.	No. mark	% mark
1580–9	37	37	100	68	57	84
1590–9	31	30	97	81	72	89
1600–9	81	76	94	33	30	91
1610–19	57	53	93	175	160	91
1620–9				213	192	90
1630–9	147	137	93	247	222	90
1640–9	22	20	91	21	17	81
1660–9	183	161	88			
1670–9	234	203	87	279	219	78
1680–9	204	172	84	374	241	64
1690–9	28	22	79	303	158	52
1720–9	98	73	74	153	67	44

Source: Cressy (1980, p.144). Reproduced by permission of Professor David Cressy.

Table 5   Occupational illiteracy of female deponents in northern England and Lowland Scotland, 1640–1770

	England		**Scotland**	
	1640–99	1700–70	1640–99	1700–70
Prof. & Gentry	(17) 24	(10) 0	(16) 35	(63) 25
Craft & Trade	(60) 78	(94) 69	(35) 71	(251) 72
Farmer Tenant	(24) 88	(31) 68	(1) 100	(42) 86
Labourer	(20) 95	(24) 88	(5) 100	(40) 90
Servant	(39) 85	(51) 75	(52) 92	(214) 88
Total	(160)	(210)	(109)	(610)

The figures in round brackets are numbers sampled, those unbracketed are percentages illiterate.

Houston (1985, p.60). Reproduced by permission of Dr R.A. Houston.

Discussion   It is impossible to make straight comparisons between the three countries. Only Tables 1 and 4 provide statistics for women for the same period, the final decade of the seventeenth century (except for Rheims), and we have no information about their status or occupation. We first have to convert the English illiteracy rates into figures for literacy by subtracting the percentages from 100. We can suggest that female literacy in Aix-en-Provence, 13%, was lower than Norfolk/Suffolk where it was 21% in 1690–9. But Aix is a town, in Norfolk and Suffolk the population was overwhelmingly rural and the higher literacy of Norwich, the second largest town in England, would not have compensated for the low rural rate. Also the English sample is very small indeed, only 28 women altogether. The larger sample of London/Middlesex women had a much higher rate of literacy, 48% compared with medium sized towns and cities in France, such as Rennes, Rouen and Angers, where it was rather lower. Although the northern English and Scottish women's literacy rates cannot be directly compared with the southern English and French women, Table 5 does enable us to draw some conclusions. If you add all the categories together and divide by 5 for 1640–99, you get an average percentage of literacy of 26% for England and 20.5% for Scotland; but again notice how small some of the samples are. Female literacy levels in Lowland Scotland seem to have been rather higher than in some areas of France such as Aix-en-Provence, but are lower than both the French towns of the North and also the women of London and East Anglia.

Despite the dangers of putting too much weight on literacy statistics, and we have only looked at a small proportion of the data available, we know enough of the patterns in the seventeenth century to recognize that the written or printed word was important for all classes. Ideas, often expressed in the form of doctrinal statements or religious and political propaganda, could be equally effective in influencing those who could read but not write; probably a substantial although largely unquantifiable section of the population. Literature could be used by the state to shape opinion by confirming religious orthodoxy and encouraging compliance with government authority. Conversely, the ability to read and write, as it spread throughout society, posed a threat to the authority of church and state: a threat which could in part be met by censorship. Some attempts by states to exercise control will be considered below; but the question must first be addressed of the motivation of the large number of people who achieved literacy during the century.

Table 3, giving the proportion of men who could sign the Protestations and Covenants which were hostile to royal policy, shows a higher incidence of literacy in and around London, an area where many of the population also rejected the authority of the Anglican church. David Cressy in *Literacy and the Social Order*, is hesitant about linking high literacy levels with religious activism. Instead he prefers a formula which links literacy to social position and economic need. This is born out by the evidence from all the British statistics we have studied: the upper classes were invariably more literate than the lower, and urban rates were higher than rural. Those who needed to read and write to establish their status in society, and/or pursue a profession or trade, acquired the necessary skills. So did many good Christians who heeded the words of divines like George Swinnock: '. . .alas, the people perish for want of knowledge. And how can they know God's will that cannot read it?' (Cressy, 1980, p.3).

Table 6   The bibliothèque bleue compared with the Pepys collection

The *bibliothèque bleue* 17th to 19th centuries(?)	After Mandrou			Morin, after Martin		Pepys's chapbook collection: mainly 1680s			
	subtotal	*no.*	%	*no.*	%		*subtotal*	*no.*	%
PIOUS WORKS									
Carols and songs about saints				161	11½	Carols	1		
Instruction				?	?	Instruction	4		
Saints' lives, etc.				69	5	Death and judgement	9		
						Death-bed testaments	7		
						'Awful warnings'	4		
						Calls to repentance	9		
						Consolation	9		
						Other	3		
Bible stories and religious tracts				161	11½				
Total		*c.120*	26	391	28			46	19
POPULAR CULTURE									
Novels: adventure and romance	'few'			184	13	Novels	5		
Burlesques and parodies	c.30			24	2	Jest-books, burlesques	24		
Morals, satires on sexes, etc.				73	5	Anti-female satire	8		
						Satirical moralities	6		
Secular songs				40	3	Secular songs	17		
Theatre				74	5	Theatre	–		
Classical literature	c.10					None (see novels?)	–		
Crime	} c.30					Crime	5		
Courtship-manuals						Courtship and lovers' dialogues	16		
Death						None, see 'pious works'	–		
Total		*c.120*	26	395	28			81	34
PORTRAITS OF SOCIETY									
Trades, miseries of apprentices						Trades, miseries of apprentices	–		
Games	} c.50					Games, cards	–		
						Riddle-books, etc.	8		
						Tricks and practical jokes	2	} 13	
Education, letter-manuals				74	5	Letter-manuals	3		
Historical legends, chivalric and subchivalric novels, including any in an historical setting	c.40		9	190	14	Robin Hood, Dick Whittington, etc.	13		
						Chivalric, Arthur, etc.	11	} 34	14
						'Roman' myths	3		
						'Realistic' novels of trades, etc.	7		
Total		*c.90*	20	264	19			47	20
EVERYDAY LIFE									
Calendars and almanacs	c.44?			not included		Almanacs	45		
Arithmetic and spelling				36	3	Arithmetic	–		
Medicine	} 20					Medicine	1		
Itineraries						Itineraries (in almanacs)	?		
Gardening						Gardening	–		
Cookery	} 6			42	3	Cookery	4		
Blacksmiths						Blacksmiths	–		
Law	–					Law	1		
Black and white magic	10			75	5	Dreams, palmistry, prognostication, etc.	12		
Newssheets, satirical pieces, politics				80	6				
Total		*c.80*	17	233	17			63	27
FAIRY MYTHOLOGY									
Fairy stories				76	6	Fairy stories	–		
'Grands mythes', Fortunatus etc.						'Grands mythes', Fortunatus	1		
Total		*c.50*	11	76	6			1	–
GRAND TOTAL		*c.460*	100	1359	98			238	100

Source: Spufford (1982, pp.136–7).

For some people the main motive for learning to read seems to have been pleasure rather than religion or profit. This is confirmed by the very considerable number of small, cheap books, pamphlets and broadsheets which were available for purchase throughout the century in France and the British Isles. In the former a higher proportion of Huguenots than Catholics were literate; should we infer from this that religion was a motivating factor in the acquisition of literacy, or was it simply a reflection of the fact that many French Protestants were engaged in commerce and industry?

Exercise   Look at Table 6 and compare the works listed by Samuel Pepys (mainly 1680s) and the 'bibliothèque bleue' (little books published at Troyes, France, from the seventeenth to the nineteenth centuries). What similarities and differences can you identify between popular reading in England and in France? ('After Mandrou' refers to the study made by Professor Robert Mandrou of the bibliothèque bleue. 'Morin after Martin' refers to later work on the same material.)

Discussion   Your first caveat is likely to be that you cannot make a straight comparison. The 'bibliothèque bleue' material is drawn from a long period, over two hundred years, the Pepys collection was made in the late seventeenth century, although some of the books would have originated in an earlier period. The 'bibliothèque bleue', collection contained 1359 works, the Pepys only 238 and this could also distort your findings.

Yet despite some necessary reservations, the comparison proves illuminating if we look at the five categories of works distinguished by Spufford in her study of the Pepys collection. Pious books were very popular in France: 28 per cent of the whole collection, and contained a high proportion of carols and songs about saints. These were absent from the Protestant books of England where a large proportion of the 19 per cent of pious works were devoted to aspects of death and repentance. This difference reflects in part the ambivalent attitude that some English Protestants had towards the role of music in religious services.

Books for entertainment were important in both countries: 28 per cent in France, 34 per cent in England and in some cases there was a taste for similar genres: gender based satire and courtship themes, for example. (Incidentally, English satires were already singling out national stereotypes for ridicule. Tales about the supposed folly of the Welsh were popular.) The English were more interested in burlesques than the French but less enthusiastic about novels offering adventure and romance. Both nations liked books about the trades and games and were equally enthusiastic about chivalric tales, 14 per cent each in this category.

When it came to books about everyday life, the English emerge as more interested in almanacs and dreams, palmistry and prognostication. It is strange that there is no record of news sheets, satirical pieces or political literature, whilst the French had 80 of these items. We know that such literature circulated in seventeenth-century England, so we must conclude that Pepys did not acquire any for his collection. Finally, the English (or Pepys) appeared to be uninterested in the fairy stories and myths which comprised 6 per cent of French reading matter.

My general conclusion from this evidence would be, given the reservations expressed in the first paragraph and that Pepys's collection reflects the taste of one man, whilst the 'bibliothèque bleue' does not, that there were quite close similarities between English and French popular taste. Where it diverged, over religious reading matter, for example, it did so because of identifiable cultural differences.

So far we have been concentrating on cultural areas which involved either the whole of society or the common people: the extent of literacy and education. Many of the institutions produced to enhance the latter were inevitably the preserve of the intellectual and economic élite who could take the lead in supporting the government of the day or in subverting it.

'Salons', academies and learned societies

We have discussed the diversity of educational opportunity available in France and the British Isles and the slow but steady increase in the number of men and women who were literate. Important factors in furthering literacy and education were religion and the state. Provided they could control the way in which education was received, church authorities and monarchs could use it as a means of producing useful, obedient and orthodox members of society. Nobles in both states, lawyers and rich bourgeois in France and gentry, professionals and rich merchants in Britain could not be readily manipulated. The civil wars and Frondes, both led by such people, demonstrated this very clearly. As we have seen above, literacy and educational attainment were increasing among the upper classes in both states. The century saw the development of several kinds of institutions which were vehicles for their values and aspirations and which had considerable cultural and political significance.

Academies were not a new phenomenon in France; Yates (1947) gives a comprehensive account of the private academies which flourished during the last years of Valois rule. They represented a counter balance to the violence of the Wars of Religion, offering the reasoned pleasures of philosophy, music, dance and poetry to an élite which could easily have become brutalised. The advent of the unrefined but successful Bourbon monarch, Henri IV, co-incided with the demise of most of the academies apart from a few riding establishments. It was left to his son and to Richelieu to encourage the foundation of new ones which were to be of a very different character to the earlier academies: they were promoted by the state and served its purposes.

Figure 5
Pluvinel's Riding
Academy, *engraving from*
A. de Pluvinel, Maneige
Royal, 1624, Paris.
Bibliothèque Nationale de
France, Paris.

Exercise   Look at Figure 5, which portrays Pluvinel's riding academy in Paris. Louis XIII is seated in the foreground and the author is standing talking to him. What values would this picture have conveyed?

Discussion   An atmosphere of order and classical decorum pervades the picture. It is framed by columns with Corinthian capitals supporting a richly ornamented entablature bearing, in the centre, the royal arms. The riding school appears to be held under an open portico adjacent to a spacious courtyard surrounded by fine buildings. All the participants in the scene are elegantly dressed and their postures suggest refinement. The rider and the bystanders to his left look like noble pupils of the Academy, the man wielding the whip is a riding master, those who, with Pluvinel, accompany the king, are probably courtiers.

The picture could be seen as an affirmation of the traditional role of the nobility as military leaders skilled in horsemanship and arms, but it also placed those skills into a context of classical culture and restraint. Most important of all, the whole process was presented to the French people as emanating from royal patronage and taking place under royal control, symbolized by the presiding coat of arms as well as the actual presence of the king.

Richelieu, a pupil of Pluvinel, reinforced state interest in the academies. During the 1630s he created a number of scholarships to enable poor young nobles to attend one of the Parisian academies.

Exercise   Read *Anthology*, II.2.

In what ways does Richelieu's description of how an academy should operate represent a development from Pluvinel's Riding Academy?

Discussion   The first few lines presumably describe what went on at most contemporary academies, the only skills which were taught were practical and were intended to make the pupils into good soldiers. Notice, incidentally, that Richelieu accepted that non-noble youths would also attend: he did not object to this provided that the nobles pursued a more intellectually rigorous curriculum. This would extend the Pluvinel model by embracing philosophy, the French language, map reading, geography and ancient and modern history as well as the military arts. In the emphasis he placed on this last subject, Richelieu seemed anxious to train future public servants – ministers and diplomats – as well as military leaders.

Richelieu's most spectacular intervention in the world of learning was the foundation of the Académie Française in 1634. An informal group of scholars including Nicholas Faret and Guez de Balzac (see Block 1, Unit 2 and Block 3, Unit 11) had been meeting, as discreetly as possible to avoid official interference, to discuss and criticize literature. When the cardinal got wind of it he made them an offer which they did not dare to refuse. He gave the Académie its official title, fixed the membership at twenty seven and added 'tone' by proposing several of his own counsellors of state. From then onwards its members served the purposes of the government, writing speeches for Richelieu and regularly voicing praise of the king and his policies. Its main objective, however, was to improve the quality of the French language, standardize its usage and promote it as the international medium of cultural exchange. The principal means of achieving these goals was the creation of a dictionary which it took the remainder of the century to produce. This was a departure from the earlier academies which were educational institutions.

Other academies for the arts and sciences were established: the one for Painting and Sculpture, was not initially directly sponsored by the state. Colbert revived it with a brief to standardize the rules for those arts in the same way that they had been established for the French language. Colbert also emulated Richelieu in making a nucleus of French scientists who gathered around Father Mersenne, a disciple of Descartes, into the Academy of Sciences. Colbert completed his work by founding academies to regulate architecture and dancing and to encourage practitioners to achieve the highest quality in their work. The state-founded academies became the custodians of fixed national standards in the arts and sciences. And statesmen (as we have seen in TV6) also used their private patronage to promote education in colleges and universities.

Women had been active in the academies of the late sixteenth century, but the martial character of those founded on the Pluvinel model excluded them. At this time, an alternative for women of spirit and intelligence was pioneered by Catherine de Vivonne, Marquise de Rambouillet who held a *salon* in her grand Parisian hôtel (mansion) between 1617 and 1665. A *salon* was a meeting of cultivated people at the house of a lady for the purpose of conducting witty and well-informed conversation.

Blue was an innovation in the 1620s, as rooms had usually been dark red or rusty brown under the Valois. Eight Flemish tapestries of classical figures standing in porticos, a gift of Louis XIII, made the room appear larger than it was. A Turkish rug covered the centre of the floor, while a kind of red satin day-bed, Chinese and Spanish chests, and chairs and folding stools lined the walls. Delft and Chinese vases, Venetian glass, and fresh flowers completed the decor. Discreetly hidden behind a tapestry, a tiny cabinet, sumptuously decorated, provided a place for the Marquise to rest with one or two intimate friends even while her 'salon' was crowded with guests. (Ranum 1968 p.153)

Figure 6
Paul Merivart, The Salon of the Marquise de Rambouillet, *Paris, engraving. Photo: Mansell Collection.*

Madamoiselle de Scudery and Madame de Sévigné attended the *salon* at the Hôtel de Rambouillet and, like other cultivated women, went on to hold their own. Contemporaries coined the term *précieuse* for such people, originally with the intention of ridiculing clever women. Yet the *salon* remained, until the French Revolution at the end of the next century, one of the pivots of reasonable and cultivated society, and did much to vindicate the proposition that men and women were intellectual equals.

Exercise The career of the Duchess of Chevreuse (herself a *précieuse*), described in Unit 2, exemplified the difficulties women encountered when they tried to achieve political power. Were the *salons* likely to give those who held and attended them any influence over contemporary affairs?

Discussion Madame de Rambouillet held a *salon* throughout the reign of Louis XIII and well into that of his son. She sported a gift from the king in her Blue Chamber. Almost all the great nobles (including Richelieu) and artists of the time attended her *salon* and you know enough of French politics to see that this would only have been possible with royal approval. On the other hand, several of the greatest ladies who held *salons* were enthusiastic supporters of the Frondes. In either case, those who held or attended *salons*, do seem to have exercised some influence over contemporary affairs.

Many of the ideas about religion, literature and politics which were to contribute to the genesis of the 'Enlightenment' emanated from the *salons* of the seventeenth and early eighteenth centuries. Their influence amongst the élite, who were privileged to attend, extended beyond France as cultivated foreigners, including British nobles and gentlemen, visited them as part of their sightseeing in Paris. Their impact on élite opinion can be contrasted with the influence of books and pamphlets which extended to all levels of society.

The British Isles during the first part of the seventeenth century produced no equivalent to the *salons* and, until the advent of the Commonwealth, little that could be compared to the French academies. Both James I and Charles I were well educated but they tended to view innovation in learning with suspicion.

The Stuarts were prepared, however, to contemplate novelty in the Arts. Charles I's patronage of painting has been referred to in Unit 2; also his belief that the powerful image of royalty, which could be conveyed by art, was of considerable importance. The foundation of the tapestry works at Mortlake was another example of direct royal intervention in the arts, although the aim was also economic: to prevent the import of some luxury goods from abroad. They were initiated by James in 1619 and drew on the skills of a colony of Flemish artists. Their finest pieces, some designed to praise the monarchy, were produced during the reign of his son. Subsequent rulers were less generous in their patronage and the works finally closed during the reign of William III. In the world of learning, however, the Stuarts expected obedience rather than innovation from the Anglican dons of Oxford and Cambridge.

Ironically, the most prominent Englishman to anticipate a new order achieved through learning ('the Great Instauration' as he called it), was Francis Bacon, a devoted servant to James I despite charges of bribery made against him in 1621. His eventual downfall was not brought about by his reformist ideas but by political intrigue at court and the hostility of parliament. His intellectual legacy, only appreciated by a few scientists and philosophers, passed to the Puritan scholars of the next generation. During the civil wars of the 1640s they saw their opportunity to break free from the supervision of the royal government.

Exercise   Read this extract from Charles Webster's *The Great Instauration*. What were to be the principal features of 'The Great Instauration'?

> . . .millenarianism [belief in Christ's second coming] played a considerable part in moulding the Puritan conception of the Great Instauration. Science was pursued not as an end in itself, but for its value in confirming the power of providence and for its applicability to social amelioration. The Puritan reformers diagnosed the deficiencies of current knowledge and sought solutions to all fundamental intellectual and social problems; in order to make headway with this ambitious programme, an essentially new attitude to knowledge was called for. It would be necessary for individuals to dedicate themselves in a totally disinterested manner to a great collaborative enterprise. The philosophies of Bacon and Comenius [an educational reformer from Bohemia], provided initial guidance ... Through the development of their ideas a new philosophy could be evolved which would be consistent with the spiritual enlightenment of the Puritans. Through universal education the young could be protected from the evils of pagan scholasticism [medieval Christian scholarship thought by progressives to be ill-informed] and be exposed to a genuine Christian philosophy. Experimental medicine could solve the problems of disease; agricultural innovation could restore the plenty of a Garden of Eden; general economic reform might bring undreamed of prosperity and elevate Britain to a position of world supremacy. (Webster, 1975, p.30)

Discussion   Your first thoughts might be that this is a secondary source and that Webster asserts that the 'Great Instauration' existed as a practical educational and social project. To be convinced by his argument we would need to read the whole book and other primary and secondary works as well. To avoid doing that, let us assume, for the purposes of this exercise, that, the Great Instauration was taken seriously by contemporary scholars and that Webster describes it accurately.

The principal features of the Great Instauration were:

1   Its connection with millenarianism: the belief that the programme would usher in a golden age on earth when truth and harmony would reign.

2   A philosophy would be developed which rejected the stale, discredited ideas of scholasticism as well as popular pagan beliefs and erroneous Christian practices.

3   Advances in knowledge would be based on observation and experiment rather than on reference to ancient authorities.

4   Society as a whole would benefit from these advances by the universal education of the young.

5   The Instauration would make England economically, politically (and by implication) morally supreme.

The body of Webster's book is devoted to a review of scientific and medical learning during the civil wars and the Interregnum and to an assessment of how far the ideals of the reformers were realized. He concedes that, until Royalist Oxford fell to parliament, work continued to be done there. He also allows that the scientific achievements of the decade before the Restoration were not nearly as notable as the work of men like Boyle and Newton which followed it.

You will probably see where this is leading: did the foundation of the Royal Society in 1660 represent a departure from the work of the Puritans in London, Oxford and Cambridge or did it build on their achievements? Writers like Hall (1972) preferred to look to the continental tradition of Galileo, Kepler and Descartes for the origins of the Royal Society rather than at home-grown talent.

Exercise   Read Coward, pp. 466–9.

1   What account does he give of the origins of the Royal Society?

2   How far can the foundation and early work of the Royal Society be seen as the product of state patronage?

Discussion   1   Coward recognizes the difficulty of making a clear connection between the Royal Society and the groups of scientists from London, Oxford and Cambridge who met in the 1650s in informal groups for discussion. He affirms, however, that there was a considerable amount of overlap between such groups and the scientists who resolved in 1660 to institute regular weekly meetings in London.

2   There seems to have been little state patronage connected with the foundation of the Royal Society. Beyond a good-natured and gentlemanly interest which extended to granting a royal charter, Charles II can be given little credit. The *virtuosi* members of the leisured classes who supported scientific activity at various levels, did so out of interest or because it was fashionable.

At the beginning of the seventeenth century most aspects of higher education and intellectual activity in the British Isles and France were controlled by the established churches. In England the slightest show of displeasure from James I could close down the first Society of Antiquaries (see Block 3, Unit 13). Archbishop Laud was able to force his brand of Anglicanism on the dons at Oxford and Cambridge. Richelieu was even more successful in gathering most forms of intellectual activity under his control and, later, Colbert emulated his example on behalf of Louis XIV. During the Frondes the potential of the *salons*, held by subversive noblewomen as political centres was briefly realized, but for most of the century the *salons* posed no real threat to royal authority.

The middle years of the century in Britain marked an advance for reform in education and learning and the momentum, especially in science, was not lost at the Restoration. The dominance of the Anglican church over the appointment of dons and the curriculum they followed, could be an inhibiting factor at Oxford and Cambridge, but generally a more liberal atmosphere prevailed, especially after 1688. English women of wit and learning never held *salons* on the scale of those in France but some, such as Locke's friend Lady Masham, certainly provided centres of political and intellectual activity. Religious toleration gradually became a tenable attitude and the balance of power between parliament and monarchy was preserved between 1688 and 1720. The degree of freedom this toleration allowed to those active in education and intellectual life was considerably greater than that enjoyed by French scholars and artists under Louis XIV, who could generally impose his will upon his subjects.

Propaganda and the press

'Propaganda' is a term which is often used in a pejorative sense in the late twentieth century. In a seventeenth-century context it should be regarded as the description of various means by which states and their churches spread officially sanctioned ideas and of the expression of their opponents' views.

Exercise   Look at Figure 7. What features of the title page would you identify which make it an effective piece of propaganda?

Discussion   The intended audience for this pamphlet, would have been to a large measure, the ordinary people who had a healthy respect for supernatural powers, not the well educated or sophisticated (though many of these still believed in supernatural phenomena). The title would do credit to a modern tabloid journalist: 'wonderful', 'miracle', 'God's just vengeance'. Negative words abound for the conduct of the unfortunate cavalier: 'blasphemous imprecations', 'distracted', 'raving' and 'blaspheming'. An air of veracity was imparted to the tale by the precise details about the cavalier: his name, his regiment and the place where the incident occurred. The list of respectable witnesses increased the credibility of the story. Finally, an air of immediacy was imparted by dating the news 'From Listelleth October the 30th, 1642,' and the pamphlet was apparently only printed nine days later. Whatever opinion might be expressed about the contents, the presentation makes it a professional and, doubtless, effective piece of propaganda.

Propaganda in one form or another is as old as politics itself and the invention of printing with movable type had long been utilized in its service. Francis I in 1534 had burnt a printer one of whose placards demanding religious reform had been tacked on to the royal bedchamber door at Amboise. Elizabeth I had not been amused by the 'Martin Marprelate' tracts which had tried to push the queen and her church closer to Calvinist practices. Governments were, on the other hand, quite capable of using printed material for their own ends. They were rather better than most subversive factions in using folk festivals and popular traditions for the same purposes. Cressy (1989) gives some graphic illustrations in his book.

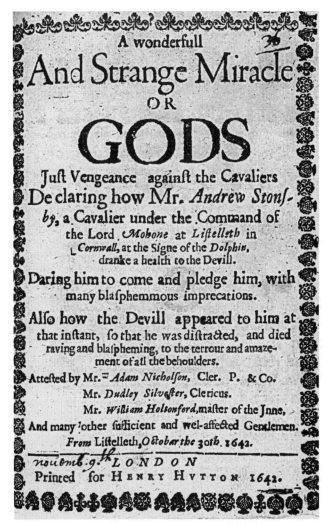

A wonderfull
And Strange Miracle
OR
GODS
Juſt Vengeance againſt the Cavaliers
Declaring how Mr. *Andrew Stonſ-*
by, a Cavalier under the Command of
the Lord *Mohone* at *Liſtelleth* in
Cornwall, at the Signe of the *Dolphin*,
dranke a health to the Devill.
Daring him to come and pledge him, with
many blaſphemmous imprecations.
Alſo how the Devill appeared to him at
that inſtant, ſo that he was diſtracted, and died
raving and blaſpheming, to the terrour and amaze-
ment of all the behoulders.
Atteſted by Mr. *Adam Nicholſon*, Cler. P. & Co.
Mr. *Dudley Silveſter*, Clericus.
Mr. *William Holtonford*, maſter of the Jnne,
And many other ſufficient and wel-affected Gentlemen.
From Liſtelleth, *Octobar the 30th.* 1642.
LONDON
Printed for H E N R Y H V T T O N 1642.

Figure 7
Title page of the pamphlet A
wonderful and strange
miracle or God's just
vengeance against
Cavaliers ..., *1642,*
London, Henry Hutton.
British Library E.126(36),
reproduced by permission of
the British Library Board.

Exercise   Read the first section of Offprint 11 and note down some examples of state propaganda at work.

Discussion   The three special days commemorating the sufferings and successes of the Stuart dynasty, all duly celebrated in royalist almanacs were: the anniversary of the execution of Charles I, Royal Oak day (Charles II's birthday and the anniversary of the Restoration) and the fifth of November (the date of the Gunpowder Plot against James I). These were supported, not only by popular demonstrations and merry-making, but also by the sermons of Anglican clergy stressing that hatred of 'papists' and other dissidents was a way of affirming loyalty to the crown.

Figure 8
Pierre Mignard, Cardinal
Mazarin, *oil on canvas.*
Musée Condé, Chantilly Inv.
N1314.
Photo: Lauros-Giraudon.

Figure 9
John Lilburne, *title-page of*
The Just Defence of
John Lilburne against such
as charge him with
turbulence of spirit, *1653,*
London. British Library
E.711(10), reproduced by
permission of the British
Library Board.

In France pro-government propaganda tended to be more decorous and less reliant on rollicking popular festivals. See Units 2 and 13 for the dignified apologies for royal policies which writers dutifully produced. Military success, whether internal or external, was an important feature of French propaganda, every battle won or city taken by Louis XIII or Louis XIV was carefully recorded for public consumption in news reports, poems, medals and engravings.

The political turmoil of the middle decades of the century both in France and the British Isles co-incided with lively and subversive propaganda campaigns. Hatred of the policies and person of Cardinal Mazarin gave rise to a genre of opposition pamphlet in France called the *Mazarinades*. These circulated freely and in considerable numbers in Paris and in larger provincial towns during the Frondes, 1648–53. Carrier (1989) has analysed the readership of these pamphlets in Grenoble. This was possible because the papers of a bookseller, Jean Nicolas, survive which record the names of his clients and the titles of some of the leaflets which they bought. Four main social groups purchased *Mazarinades*: lawyers, churchmen, gentlemen and merchants. Yet these sales only represented about one-third of the demand for contemporary political pieces, two-thirds of Nicolas's sales were declarations or letters from the king or other kinds of official publications. See Anthology, II.3 for an example of a *Mazarinade*.

In Britain subversive propaganda was produced for a much larger part of the century than was possible under the authoritarian French government. Up to the outbreak of the Bishops' Wars draconian penalties such as brandings, beatings, imprisonment and mutilation were fairly effective. Pamphlets demanding religious and political reform were published in increasing numbers from the late 1630s, but the House of Commons remained the principal voice of opposition to the monarchy. Reports of its debates and copies of the various protestations and proposals that were exchanged with Charles I, and also of the manifestos of the Covenanters in Scotland were compulsive reading for many Britons during the 1640s. Even before the execution of the king, views about the nature of religious and social organization were surfacing which were regarded as dangerous to the established order by Cromwell, the Army grandees and the majority in parliament. The ability of Levellers, Diggers, Ranters, etc. to disseminate their ideas was progressively curbed by the grandees and parliament.

Exercise   Read *Anthology,* II.4. What kinds of argument does Lilburne use to put his case?

Discussion   The title-page bears a text from the bible (in parts of the pamphlet not printed in the *Anthology* Lilburne recounted his sufferings at the hands of the authorities over recent years) so the quotation associated him with Job. The reference to the poor also concentrated on an essential part of his political agenda. The religious theme was continued throughout the pamphlet: at one point Lilburne compared his tormentors with those who persecuted Jesus Christ, leaving his readers to make the obvious connection. The concluding paragraph, after a phrase reminiscent of the Song of Solomon, (part of the Old Testament): 'I have been hunted like a Partridge upon the mountains', ended on another thoroughly biblical note: 'I know that my redeemer liveth etc.'.

Lilburne also played the sympathy card, recounting the persecution he had suffered. His incarceration in Newgate and treatment as a felon was a shameful sequel. In a direct address to his readers: '...dear Countrymen, friends, and Christians ...' he protested his innocence.

Most persuasive of all was his claim that his main political demand had always been that all men, women and children should enjoy their just inheritance of freedom. An essential characteristic of this freedom was that no one should be subjected to arbitrary imprisonment (according to Magna Carta): it was well worth suffering in order to safeguard the ancient right of the English to trial by jury.

The restoration of Charles II did not see the demise of subversive political literature and imagery although it did see the re-imposition of some of the older mechanisms of censorship. Some of the anti-Catholic propaganda described by Cressy (read Offprint 11, sections 2, and 3) was organized by Whigs like Lord Shaftesbury who wished both to limit royal power and to ensure a Protestant succession. The conflict between the critics of the Whigs and their supporters reached fever pitch in the last years of Charles II and during the reign of James II. After the Revolution of 1688 the profusion and cheapness of printed papers led to something of a publishing explosion. About four hundred copies a time of the journal *The Review* were published, and a thousand of *The Spectator*. Copies were available in coffee houses and were circulated in taverns so the views they contained were widely disseminated, at least in London. In 1702 the first daily paper, *The Daily Courant* appeared, followed four years later by *The Evening Post*.

The Tories seem to have been the first to realize the potential of the growing market for newspapers and journals. Robert Harley, later Earl of Oxford, gathered together a formidable team of journalists, including John Toland (see Unit 13), Daniel Defoe and Dean Swift to promote his policies. They were particularly effective in mobilizing public opinion against Godolphin and Marlborough who were associated with the policy of continuing the war with France. In 1711 Mrs Manley took over from Swift as editor of *The Examiner*, a popular Tory journal. With the change in the political climate in 1714, the Whigs were soon to make up lost ground. Yet much of the credit for securing the freedom of expression for diverse opinions has been claimed for Harley:

> Oxford's ministry was the first to employ the techniques of opposition in office ... The overwhelming need for control through restrictions was replaced by the realisation of control through the well-timed release of official propaganda and counter-propaganda.
> (Downie, 1979, p.195)

 Now turn to AC1, section 3 for a comparative exercise on propaganda.

Censorship

Censorship is the companion of propaganda in most states. In France and Britain today nothing can be freely published which can be legally established as blasphemous, libellous or a threat to national security. The same categories existed in the seventeenth century, and powerful governments could define them in such a way as to prevent the appearance of anything that was even mildly subversive.

Exercise Read Coward, pp.238–9 and Briggs, pp.184–8. What differences existed between the freedom of expression in England and in France?

Discussion Censorship in England before the outbreak of the civil wars seems to have been fairly effective, as Coward highlights the great burst of political publications which followed the collapse of royal government. It is also clear that Cromwell and parliament shared the view that too much freedom of expression was dangerous and successfully re-imposed controls. Later in the century levels of censorship varied according the attitude of the government of the day.

In France censorship existed from the beginning of the century, but those who held unorthodox opinions were not united into an opposition and were discreet, so repression was spasmodic and largely ineffectual. During the reign of Louis XIV, it was organized more systematically: the small amount of subversive literature, which was available, was mostly smuggled in from abroad.

As an orthodox Catholic state France was subject to religious censorship of printed matter in the form of the Papal Index: a list of books prohibited by the Catholic church. The Anglican church, even under Laud's regime, never achieved absolute control over English religious publications. The career of William Alexander, Earl of Stirling, discussed in Unit 2 illustrates the difficulties encountered in Scotland when attempts were made to impose an Anglican service book.

Opposition to censorship on doctrinal grounds was no new phenomenon, although those who deplored the controls exercised by the Catholic church or Anglican prelates were often equally intolerant of views which were contrary to their own beliefs. By the middle of the seventeenth century, enlightened opinion in the British Isles and France was moving towards the view that censorship was wrong in itself as it imposed an unreasonable restraint on personal liberty.

Exercise Read *Anthology*, II.5, 6. What arguments against censorship does each writer put forward?

Discussion

Figure 10
John Milton, *engraving by William Faithorne, 1670. National Portrait Gallery, London.*

Figure 11
Pierre Bayle, *engraving by Louis Petit. Photo: Roger-Viollet.*

Milton used the example of Catholic scholars and Arminius, whose ideas had influenced the Anglican church under Archbishop Laud, to show that dangerous doctrines in books were more potent in the hands of the learned than the ignorant. Since the former could not be prevented from reading such literature and from influencing the masses, it would be futile to try and control ordinary people by censorship. Those who were responsible for implementing it would be as liable to error or corruption as anyone else. Milton's final argument was imbued with nationalist fervour: the English enjoyed access to a greater measure of truth than less fortunate nations, especially the Islamic Turks. The reformation of religion, in defiance of the pope and his prelates, could be attributed to that freedom. Yet there was no justification for complacency and these precious advantages had to be defended and extended.

Whilst Milton was deeply concerned with freedom to express ideas about religion, Bayle, in this extract, concentrated on writings which were proscribed for obscenity. He listed nine reasons an author might have for producing material which was obscene. Cunningly, the first reason was presented as being full of depravity and intended to corrupt others. Bayle could then claim some moral high ground by condemning it robustly. Reasons two to eight simply described the way in which various authors had dealt with obscene material in the past and Bayle assumed a neutral position. He did, however, distinguish between works such as Margaret of Navarre's *Heptameron* which did not deserve rigorous condemnation and the *Raggionamenti* of Leonardo Arentino which did. He also pointed out that the pressure of opinion from other writers was a much more effective control on profane writers than the use of legislation. The most acceptable kind of work which contained obscenities was the sort that Bayle produced in which 'filthy and immodest' material, by earlier writers, was cited and then condemned.

The description given by Briggs (pp.187–8) of the changing intellectual climate in France during the later part of our period, and especially the growth of Parisian *salons* and private patronage which rivalled court-dominated culture, implies that official censorship was not totally effective. In the long run, the philosophers of the Enlightenment, some of whom actually supported strong monarchical institutions, would prove more subversive of state authority than the few obscure writers and printers who dared to defy the monarchy and were duly crushed.

In England after the Restoration a series of Licensing Acts (1662–95) preserved the control of the royal ministers over books about history and politics; the Anglican church had the power to suppress any unwelcome works about philosophy, divinity or science. In the more liberal atmosphere of the reigns of William and Mary and of Anne the Licensing Acts were allowed to lapse and in 1712 a Stamp Act levied a tax on newspapers and journals. This at least left the middle and upper classes, who could afford to pay the tax, freedom of access to controversial religious and political literature.

Conclusion

The freedom to express personal beliefs about religion and politics, and the attempt of states and churches to impose an official view of these matters through propaganda and censorship is a large subject and we have only touched on some aspects of it. A concluding exercise draws together some of the points which have been made above.

Exercise What similarities and differences can be identified between the way in which the state and the churches and their opponents communicated views about religion, society and politics in Britain and France during the seventeenth century?

Discussion Let's take similarities first: we seem to be dealing with populations educated to roughly the same level, most of the male members of the upper classes were literate, as were the middle classes/bourgeoisie by the end of the period. Higher literacy rates prevailed at all levels in the towns than in the country and amongst men than amongst women. Evidence survives that a market existed in the lower orders of society for ballads, etc. so we can infer that a large potential market also existed both for government and for subversive propaganda. In both states official churches claimed the authority to define the religious beliefs the population were allowed to hold, and the churches were to an important extent, dependent on the support of the monarchy.

Differences arose when political history, and with it the degree of control which the states and their churches were capable of exercising, diverged after the 1630s. After the Frondes the French monarchy reasserted its authority and its power to dominate all major forms of education and the communication of culture within the country. Unparalleled freedom existed for a few years within Britain and anarchy prevailed in Ireland, during which time all manner of ideas were expressed. Controls were eventually restored, but the hold the Anglican church and the later Stuarts exercised over peoples' minds was never unquestioned. The Revolution of 1688 permanently established a more liberal atmosphere for the exchange of ideas about church and state.

References

Canny, N.(1982), 'The Foundation of the Irish Mind: Religion, Politics and Gaelic Irish Literature, 1580–1750', *Past and Present*, 95, pp.91–116.

Carrier, H. (1989), *La Presse de la Fronde (1648–1653), Les Mazarinades: La Conquête de l'Opinion*, Histoire et Civilisation du Livre, Geneva.

Chartier, R., Compère, M.M., Julia, D. (1976), *L' Education en France du XVI au XVIII siècle*, Paris.

Cressy, D. (1980), *Literacy and the Social Order: Reading and Writing in Tudor and Stuart England*, Cambridge University Press, Cambridge.

Cressy, D. (1989), *Bonfires and Bells: National Memory and the Protestant Calendar in Elizabethan and Stuart England* University of California Press, Berkeley.

Downie, J.A. (1979), *Robert Harley and the Press: Propaganda and Public opinion in the Age of Swift and Defoe*, Cambridge University Press, Cambridge.

Hall, A.R. (1972), 'Science, Technology and Utopia in the Seventeenth Century', in P. Mathias (ed.) *Science and Society, 1600–1900*, Cambridge University Press, Cambridge.

Houston, R.A. (1985), *Scottish Literacy and the Scottish Identity: Illiteracy and Society in Scotland and Northern England*, 1600–1800, Cambridge University Press, Cambridge.

Lougée, C.C. (1976), *Le Paradis des Femmes: Women, Salons and Social Stratification in Seventeenth Century France*, Princeton University Press, Princeton, N.J.

O'Day, R. (1982), *Education and Society, 1500–1800: the Social Foundation of Education in Early Modern Britain*, Longman, London.

Ranum, O. (1968), *Paris in the Age of Absolutism*, Wiley, New York.

Schimmelpenninck, M.A. (1813), *Narrative of a Tour in the Year 1667 to La Grande Chartreuse and Alet by Dom Claude Lancelot*, London.

Spufford, M. (1981), *Small Books and Pleasant Histories: Popular Fiction and its Readership in Seventeenth Century England*, Methuen, London.

Webster, C. (1975), *The Great Instauration*, Duckworth, London.

Yates, F. (1947), *French Academies of the Sixteenth Century*, Warburg Institute, London.

Unit 7
Religion and dissent

Prepared for the course team by Bill Sheils

Contents

Study timetable

Weeks of Study	Texts	Video	AC	Set books
2	Unit 7; *Anthology*, II. 8–14; Offprint 12	7		Coward, Briggs

Objectives

The objectives of this unit are to introduce you to:

1   the variety of religious loyalties that existed within the countries as a result of the Reformation and Counter Reformation changes of the previous century;

2   the problems which that variety caused for governments, and the measures they took to deal with them;

3   the way in which religion was perceived by both leading laymen and clergy, and by the people that they governed and instructed;

4   the way in which religion influenced the people, both in the matter of worship and in their everyday lives.

Religious divisions and problems of authority 1620–60

Russell (1990) wrote that the trouble with England in 1637 was that it was a country of several religions with a structure that was only designed to have one. This statement is true, not only of England and Wales; but also of Scotland and Ireland at this time. It was generally the case in Protestant Europe that independent political units, be they cities like Geneva or countries such as England, sustained an established church order within their boundaries which did not include toleration of other native religious groups, although refugee churches from other countries, such as the Huguenot community at Canterbury, were permitted a degree of freedom of worship according to their native traditions. In England the Reformation had been piece-meal and prolonged and in certain parts of the country, most notably in the north and in London, vigorous, if small, pockets of Catholicism survived. These were served by Jesuit and other missionary priests who had been sent abroad by their parents for their training, and had an ambivalent attitude to secular authority. They had been implicated in treasonous activity as recently as 1605 in the Gunpowder Plot but also recognized that their best hope for a return to Catholicism in the nation, or for toleration of their beliefs, lay in the support they might get from the king or his chief advisers.

Among the Protestants there were also divisions, the most important being between the defenders of the Established Church, consisting of bishops, archdeacons, cathedral clergy, and some parish ministers on the one side, and the Puritans, mostly parish ministers, schoolmasters and preachers or lecturers, with support from some theologians at the universities, on the other. They also had a following among those members of the gentry in parliament who sought a further reform of ecclesiastical structures more closely identified with the sort of church order found in Calvinist countries abroad. Each group subscribed to a Calvinist theology, though differences of emphasis existed concerning the central doctrine of grace, predestination. Their shared theology, and the perceived threat from hostile Catholic countries, meant that almost all Protestants, whilst vigorously pursuing their own religious objectives, remained wedded to the notion of a national church and were bound by common concerns in the defence of the nation against Anti-Christ, who in their eyes was personified by the pope. However, the differences between these groups were sharpened by the bishops in the 1620s when Arminian views (see Coward, pp.112–13, 172–3) emerged among a powerful group of churchmen around William Laud, who was appointed bishop of London in 1626 and archbishop of Canterbury in 1633. As a consequence of this new theology, such consensus as had existed between bishops and Puritans, and which had kept most of the latter within the Established Church, started to break down. Increasing numbers began to withdraw from the church, if not completely then at least into 'godly' gatherings in which they could pursue their more rigorous devotional life. Despite their dissatisfaction with the bishops, most of these Puritans still believed that the church should be a national church, embracing all inhabitants, and therefore sought to reform the institution from within. A minority, however, sustained by the Calvinist doctrine of election, in which those predestined to be saved from the beginning of time, the elect, were separated spiritually from the rest of humanity, the damned, cut themselves off completely from what they saw as a compromised and ungodly church. Instead they joined together in 'gathered, separatist' congregations which were independent of other churches. In addition, during the 1630s a few congregations took themselves to New England, where they could attempt to establish their version of the Reformation without the constraining interference of an unsympathetic hierarchy. You should now read Coward, pp.127–33.

We will now turn to Scotland where the Reformation had been swifter and more dramatic and a Book of Discipline, erecting a Presbyterian form of church government with elected ministers, assisted by lay elders and deacons serving the parishes, was adopted by parliament in 1581. The wider governance of the church was entrusted to regional sessions and a national general assembly led by a moderator, elected from among his fellow ministers, was established as the chief authority. This would have placed the Scottish experience within the broad spectrum of the European Calvinist tradition, had the proposal gained universal support, but even here compromise was needed. James VI was no lover of the kirk and in the 1580s a few Presbyterians had been forced into exile in England. James preferred episcopacy, with its more hierarchical and less 'democratic' structures, and in 1610 had persuaded the general assembly to approve the restoration of most of the bishops' jurisdiction. Thus the Scottish church also was in two minds about its true nature, and this was to prove important in the 1630s under Charles I, who lacked the political skill of his father. Moreover, despite the achievements of the Protestants there were parts of the country, especially in the Highlands, where the Reformation had made very little impact, so that a reservoir of traditional pre-Reformation religion survived at odds with the religious ambitions of the reformers, and further separated from them by a culture which was predominantly Gaelic speaking.

The Reformation in Ireland had been largely an institutional affair, or one that had been transplanted by settlers from England in the reign of Elizabeth, and from Scotland early in the seventeenth century. As such it had hardly touched the hearts of the indigenous population outside of the major towns. Furthermore, those who brought the Reformation to Ireland were often of a Puritan persuasion, like Walter Travers the first principal of Trinity College, Dublin (founded 1592), or were Presbyterian Scots unsympathetic to the episcopal church established by parliament and staffed by poorly paid, and often absentee, bishops and clergy. In Ireland therefore the religious divisions of the country were aggravated by ethnic and linguistic differences between the peoples that made up the nation; the Gaelic-speaking natives and the 'Old English' who had settled there during the middle ages on the Catholic side, and the recently arrived Protestant settlers from England and Scotland.

In France the situation was somewhat different in that the country was Catholic and therefore part of the universal church rather than an independent ecclesiastical entity. The crown sought and achieved a considerable measure of independence from the papacy in the matter of patronage within the French church, but matters of doctrine and belief lay outside the remit of the national institutions. Although Catholic at the start of our period France had undergone a series of Wars of Religion during the previous century which had threatened the authority of the crown and which were only brought to an end by the accession of Henri IV (1589–1610), himself a Protestant who became a Catholic to secure the throne (the famous saying 'Paris is worth a Mass' is his). In 1598, through the Edict of Nantes, he granted toleration to his former co-religionists, the Huguenots, who had established congregations in many of the important regional towns, such as Bordeaux. Henri was himself assassinated in 1610 and toleration proved to be difficult to enforce on regional authorities unsympathetic to the Protestants. At the very beginning of our period the young king of France, Louis XIII, was leading an army against the Protestants in Béarn in the south-west corner of the kingdom, laying siege to their fortresses, many of which were burned following the Treaty of Montpellier in 1622.

Thus the religious map of each country in 1620 was far from uniform and even in France, where toleration was formally decreed, differences in religion posed serious practical problems for a government wishing to sustain peace and order in particular provinces within the realm. The problems were not only practical, however, but conceptual, in that they were concerned with questions of authority in church and state. These questions became particularly important in Britain during the 1630s when the crown attempted to govern without parliament in England, and also found itself, in the person of King Charles I, with responsibilities to two differing religious traditions, episcopacy in England and Presbyterianism in Scotland. This anomalous position was difficult enough, but affairs in England, where the Arminian churchmen sought to restore the rights of the clergy against the laity in matters of patronage and to re-order the liturgy and the architectural arrangement of the churches, aroused hostile opposition.

Exercise   Read Coward, pp.172–8 and list the elements in Laud's policy which seemed most threatening to the Puritans and their lay patrons.

Discussion   I would include in this list:

1   the moving of the communion table to the east end of the church;

2   the attack on preachers;

3   the introduction of games on the sabbath;

4   the challenge to lay patronage in the church.

There may be others which you think just as important. While, individually, each of these changes was contentious, in combination they appeared to threaten the very basis of the Protestant reformation, especially as the court was suspected of having Catholic sympathies.

You should now read *Anthology*, II.8, noting any phrases which indicate that Laud and the king were conscious of the way in which their policies had caused problems. Both are clearly very sensitive to the rumours of papist tendencies and, in trying to distance themselves from 'such brain-sick jealousies' they appear to the modern reader to protest too much.

You should also bear in mind what the text has to say about the nature of political and ecclesiastical authority. The canons were decided by Convocation, the senior legislative body of the church and one composed entirely of clergy, among whom the bishops had the dominant voice. As you will see from the heading they were promulgated by the king's authority, this was because they were rejected by parliament as Figure 12 suggests.

This Canons seal'd, well forg'd, not made of lead,
Give fire, O noe, I will breake and strike us dead.

That I S.B. doe sweare that I doe approve the Doctrine and Discipline or Government established in the Church of *England*, as containing all things necessary to Salvation; And that I will not endeavour by my selfe or any other, directly or indirectly to bring in any Popish Doctrine, contrary to that which is so established: Nor will I ever give my consent to alter the Government of this Church, by Archbishops, Bishops, Deanes, and Arch-Deacons, &c. as it stands now established, and as by right it ought to stand: Nor yet ever to subject it to the usurpations and superstitions of the Sea of Rome. And all these things I doe plainly and sincerely acknowledge and sweare, according to the plain and common sence, and understanding of the same words, without any equivocation or mentall evasion, or secret reservation whatsoever. And this I doe heartily, willingly and truly, upon the faith of a Christian: So help me God in Iesus Christ.

Prime, lay the Trayne, thus you must mount, and levell,
    then shall we gett the day. *but freind the Devill.*
Turne, wheele about, take tyme, and stand your ground,
    this Canon cannot faile, *but 'tis not sound,*
Feare not, weel cast it, 'tis a desperate case,
    weel sweare it, and enjoyne it, *but 'tis base,*
The Mettalls brittle, and 'tis ram'd so hard,
    with an *Oath* &c: that hath fowly marr'd
All our designes, that now we have no hope;
    but in the service of *our Lord the Pope,*
Dissolve the Rout, each man vnto his calling
    which had we kept, we had not now beene falling

Figure 12
Cartoon by W. Hollar c. 1640. In May 1640 Convocation approved new canons (laws) for the church, including the oath not to alter its government by archbishops, bishops 'etc.' (which some took to mean the pope). In December the Commons declared these canons illegal. Copyright © British Museum Department of Prints and Drawings BMC148, reproduced by permission of the Trustees.

Exercise Now read Coward, pp. 178–80 where he notes the errors made by Charles in his treatment of the Scots. Which two do you consider most important?

Discussion I think that these were:

1   His intention to revoke all grants of kirk lands made since 1540. This would have alienated the landowners who had received the grant of tithes on these lands and would now stand to lose those profits, or at least have them reduced to a fixed money payment.

2   The attempt to impose the Book of Common Prayer, which was in use in the English church, on the Scots without considering their own tradition of worship. (You will see the context of that worship in the treatment of Burntisland Church in Video 7.)

You may also have listed the fact that Charles increased the role of the bishops in secular government, and I would accept this as an alternative to my first point, but I hope that you agree that the second is crucial.

Coward then recounts briefly the disturbances in Scotland during 1637 which led to the National Covenant of 1638, which you studied in Unit 3.

You should now re-read *Anthology*, I.13 and then read *Anthology*, II.8. These two documents emerged in very different contexts: the Canons from the crown and the Covenant from a representative body of those people disaffected from the royal policy in Scotland. Both documents also refer to the uncertainties that had arisen as a result of recent policies; in the Canons Charles specifically distances the Arminian innovations from Catholicism, a *de facto* acknowledgement that many people in the country were concerned on this very point, however incorrectly. To the untutored observer the outward forms of Arminian theology, with its emphasis on the sacraments and prayer rather than on preaching, looked just like the ritual associated with Catholicism. In Scotland the covenanters, who were drawn from all sections of society, resolved to forbear the practice of all 'novations', listing especially the changes in worship and the increased status given to bishops, policies which they saw as tending to the 're-establishment of the Popish Religion and Tyranny'. (Note here that their objections are qualified by the phrase 'till they be tried and allowed in free assemblies and in Parliament'. What does that phrase tell us about the attitude of these people to religious authority?)

It is clear from the document that the defence of true religion rests with the people acting through their representative assemblies, and indeed it was in defence of that very thing that the Covenant was written.

Exercise   Look at the way in which the authors of both documents defined the role of the crown in this matter, and try and put that in your own words.

Discussion   (a) *National Covenant*
I hope that you come up with something along the following lines: The king's responsibility is made in the Coronation oath and is expressed chiefly in terms of service and of support. He is required to see that true religion, 'according to the laudable Lawes and Constitutions received in this Realme', can be practised without hindrance, and to take punitive action against all those who depart from that religion, or are identified as having done so by the church authorities, the colourful phrase is 'root out of their Empire all Hereticks'. That religion itself, however, was established by the 'great assembly', and is to be judged against scriptural authority. The king does not appear to have an independent role in matters of doctrine or church order.

(b) Canons of 1640

First, you should note that kingship is itself described as a 'sacred order', which is established both by scripture and by the laws of nature. The Canons then go on to say that the care of God's church is committed to kings, but this is glossed in an entirely different way from what was done in the National Covenant. The king is the chief governor of the church with extensive powers to call and dissolve ecclesiastical councils at will, and to override if necessary the decisions of such bodies where they are deemed prejudicial to the safety of the church, a matter on which the king seems to be the final authority.

We can see from these passages that there were two very different views as to how religion, usually expressed through the church, reacted with the state, in the person of the king, in early seventeenth-century Britain.

Although the question of the Huguenots remained decisive, the situation in France was rather different. No formal claims were made for the crown in matters of doctrine or church order at this time, and royal authority was exercised chiefly through informal methods, and in particular the control of senior appointments such as bishoprics and university professorships. In that way religion in France in the early seventeenth century was a less important source of conflict within the state than it proved to be in Britain, where Charles attempted to impose his formal powers on a resistant Calvinist tradition in two of his realms.

The suspicion of Charles's religious motives in England combined with resentment at his attempts to impose a Prayer Book on Scotland so that, when an insurrection broke out among his Catholic subjects in Ireland, these religious grievances, along with other social and political uncertainties, formed a prelude to a breakdown of that peace and order which are mentioned in both of the documents we have just discussed. The outbreak of civil war in the three kingdoms had several consequences for religion; in 1643 the English opponents of Charles combined with the Scots in a military alliance which included a Solemn League and Covenant, echoing the National Covenant of 1638, to establish Presbyterianism in England. This met with opposition in the English parliament, which feared that its authority would be undermined by the ministers, and its attitude was briskly described by one of the Scots Commissioners as follows 'The English were for a civil League, we for a religious Covenant'.

The situation in England was complex, and during the civil wars a variety of radical groups emerged which cannot easily be labelled simply as religious; they each would claim a religious impulse or motive, but their concerns ranged over a wide spectrum of social, political, and cultural questions. It is not possible to deal with these groups in any detail here, but it is important to know who they were, what common ideas they shared, and how they differed.

Exercise   Read now Coward, pp.238–68 and consider the following problems:

1   List the religious and other groups mentioned by him and try to decide from what he has written about them the extent to which their concerns were primarily religious or not.

2   What ideas were common to many of these groups?

3   Explain the concerns of the conservatives and identify one or two major worries they had about the radicals.

4   How did Cromwell's personality affect the religious experiments of his governments?

Discussion   This is a lengthy exercise with many aspects, and I imagine that we will all come up with slightly different answers. But I hope that the following will emerge.

1 (a) The Levellers contained a wide variety of religious opinions within their ranks but shared strong political beliefs broadly in line with the views expressed in the *Agreement of the People*. We shall return to the Putney Debates in Unit 13. You will remember the importance attached to religion in the extract from Lilburne which you have looked at in Unit 6.

(b)   The Diggers, led by Gerrard Winstanley, added an intellectual distrust of conventional learning to their radical political views.

2   Most of the religious groups shared a profound belief that the kingdom of God, the millennium, was imminent, and what distinguished them from each other, and indeed from more mainstream Protestant churches, was the intensity with which they held on to that belief. Most of the sects also shared a belief in the 'inner light' which transmitted to each person an understanding of religious truth and thus reduced the importance of the clergy or of a state church. This meant that many also attacked the notion of church property, espoused the cause of toleration, and defended the right of the laity to preach.

3   The views of the Quakers on the 'inner light' led many of them to place individual conscience above conventional notions of law and morality (note the quote from Clarkson in Coward, p.242), thereby antagonizing moderate opinion, which stressed order and feared moral and spiritual breakdown. The moral radicalism of the Quakers coincided with the political radicalism of the Levellers in the years immediately following the execution of the king in 1649 to the discomfort of more mainstream Puritans. Many of the leading parliamentarians were not radicals and would have shared Cromwell's view that the execution of the king was necessary rather than desirable.

4   Cromwell's character remains elusive to historians. He followed a narrow, but often wavering path between radical and conservative ideas. Three points, however, are important: he shared the millenarian ideas of many contemporaries, he held to a strong providential interpretation of his career as being guided by the hand of God, and he never renounced his commitment to religious toleration, a toleration which, in the view of one Puritan observer, would make England 'a land of saints and a pattern of holiness to the world, and the unmatchable paradise of the earth'. Cromwell was ahead of his

time in this, and even prepared to extend toleration to non-Christian religions, permitting the Jews to return in 1655, though Catholics of course remained formally excluded.

Despite these achievements, the experiments of the years following 1649 failed to resolve the vexed question of the nature of religious authority and its relationship to civil government, and in 1660 the established episcopal church was restored under the new monarch. Its doctrine and structures remained more or less intact, though some of its judicial power, exercised through the church courts, was diminished or removed. What did happen after 1660, which had not happened before, was that large numbers of Protestants chose to form their own congregations independent of the state church, notwithstanding the civil disabilities which were imposed upon them by the establishment (see Coward, pp.292–8). Thus dissent, or Nonconformity, became a part of British life.

Bringing religion to the people

Turn now to Video 7 and begin the video exercise, for much of our knowledge of what the experience of religion must have meant to the laity can be gleaned from the physical remains of the churches in which they worshipped, week in week out. I have used this last phrase quite deliberately to remind you that religion consists in patterns of behaviour as well as in matters of belief, and this was the way most contemporaries felt about it too.

Video Exercise 1   Watch Part 1 of Video 7 noting how the church furnishings at Guimilliau serve the purposes of the seventeenth-century Breton congregation and how a medieval building has been adapted to meet new requirements in the parish. The furniture is closely related to specific points of theology and to liturgical activities. The altar, pulpit, organ, font and confessional are designed to meet the sacramental, preaching, musical, baptismal and confessional functions of the church.

Video Exercise 2   Now watch Part 2 of the video, making notes on which of these functions can be seen in the Scottish Presbyterian church of Burntisland.

Discussion   The congregation is distinguished by the seats: the magistrates and the members of the guilds. The communion table is in the centre of the church, and the guild members in the galleries look down on it. The magistrates are roughly on the same level and women sat on stools, which they brought with them, on the main floor of the church, now taken up with box pews. The altar is a modest table, difficult to reach from the different parts of the church, suggesting that the administration of the sacraments at the table was not an important part of the church's activity. The communion table is dwarfed by the pulpit (which was originally in this position, though the pulpit itself is modern). It was preaching which was of the greatest importance. There was originally no organ: music was not an important part of the services and the font, for baptisms, is very unobtrusive. There is no confessional. Reformed Protestant churches placed much more emphasis on the preaching of the word than on the traditional sacraments of the Roman Catholic church.

Video Exercise 3   Now watch Part 3 of the video and make notes on how the religious functions of the church at Monnington-on-Wye are indicated in the furnishings.

Discussion   The congregation sits facing the altar at the east end, but it also has a clear view of the pulpit and reading desk (from which the prescribed lessons from the Bible were read). The main congregation can also see the local gentry in their pew next to the screen. The altar is a simple table, but it is placed against the east wall and is separated from the body of the church both by rails and by steps, as well as the screen. The pulpit is in a prominent position, and would have been more conspicuous before it was reduced in height. There is no organ or confessional. The font is at the rear of the church but it is a prominent piece of furniture and was plainly seen as a necessary part of the rebuilding of the church in 1679.

This is a church where preaching is important, but so is the celebration of communion. Communicants are expected to go up to the altar and receive the sacraments from the magnificent communion plate, kneeling at the altar rail. This was the form of communion which was established by the Elizabethan church settlement and to which Puritans had most strenuously objected; they wanted something much more like the arrangement at Burntisland. The church settlement which accompanied the restoration of the monarchy in 1660 largely reinstated the Elizabethan settlement and was enforced by a series of visitations by bishops to enquire into the state of the churches and clergy in their dioceses. (See, for example, the Visitation Articles in the *Anthology* (II.14).)

Video Exercise 4   Make notes comparing the similarities and differences between the furnishings of the churches of Burntisland and Monnington-on-Wye and their significance for the different functions. Now watch Part 4 of the video for the discussion.

This is an appropriate point at which to move from questions of authority and of worship and to consider the way in which religion was perceived by some individuals, and how they thought it could best be made available to the population at large. The sources which historians use for this are varied and those which have been chosen are designed to illustrate that variety, as well as to represent differing theological traditions.

Figure 13
Revd Richard Baxter,
engraving after Robert White.
Mary Evans Picture Library.

We have noted that, during the civil wars, a few sects emerged which challenged the idea of a clerically dominated religion, developing a theology of 'inner light' which gave the individual Christian conscience the final authority in spiritual matters. Important as they were, they were few in number. More numerous, as the complaints of clerics constantly remind us, were those who understood little and cared less, but even these expected to be baptized, married, and buried by their parish minister. More numerous still were those who fulfilled their weekly obligation to attend church, but did little beyond that, except perhaps trying to lead a decent life among their neighbours. From the committed, however, more was expected, and for Protestants especially this involved a disciplined moral piety which set them apart from the rest of the church. This is particularly strongly emphasized in the first source we shall examine, which comes from the autobiography of a leading Puritan minister in mid-seventeenth-century England, Richard Baxter.

In *Anthology*, II.9, Baxter recalls his ministry in the town of Kidderminster in the English midlands during the Interregnum. He is an important figure in the period, despite the fact that he could never reconcile himself to the execution of the king. At the Restoration it was thought that he might be a suitable candidate for a bishopric but, in the event, he was unable to accept the terms of the settlement and lived out the remainder of his long life, during which he suffered periods of imprisonment, as a dissenting minister.

Exercise   Now read *Anthology*, II.9 and try to answer the following questions.

1   What was the most important feature of that ministry, and what additional devices did he use to support it?

2   How did he measure the success of his ministry, and what circumstance did he mention especially as assisting in this?

3   What gave him most satisfaction about the results of his work in the town?

Discussion   I expect that you have a list by now, and that some of the following appear on it.

1   Preaching was clearly the central part of his ministry. He preached twice a week and supported his sermons by repetition of the themes with the more zealous of the congregation, and by discussion of the same among the younger godly of the town. This was reinforced by regular catechizing of the families of the parish in the main tenets of their faith.

2   His greatest success was the reform of the lives of the parishioners. The church had to be extended (physically as well as socially), the sabbath was kept more austerely, and even among the more dissolute families which haunted inns and alehouses there were some members who 'did seem to be religious'. Note that Baxter particularly mentioned the fact that the town was a weaving town, so that the godly could have a book before them as they worked. This reminds us of the importance of literacy for the sort of reformation which the moderate Puritan minister sought to achieve among the people.

3   He was most proud of the fact that his ministry had brought order
and peace to the town and that religious discord, and private
churches, had been overcome.

In sum we have a picture of a disciplined and earnest people, living in a
community in which the church embraced all and touched the lives of
all. It was a small godly commonwealth harmoniously set in the wider
national commonwealth, a situation which remained the ideal of the
mainstream Protestant churches. Within that godly commonwealth there
existed a spiritual hierarchy, with the more zealous of the laity gathering
together to further their knowledge of the scriptures and setting an
example of sobriety and good behaviour to their less committed neighbours. This hierarchy was related to the social hierarchy in practice, but
was not necessarily so. Such was the essence and aspiration of mainstream
Calvinism.

Anthology, II.9 is important in reminding us that, in addition to the
questions of authority that we have discussed above, the disputes between
king and parliament over religion were also about a way of life, one
which appeared to be threatened by an ecclesiastical policy which rel-
egated preaching to a subsidiary role and, with its emphasis on freewill
and on ritual, seemed to be reminiscent of Catholicism. It was this threat
to their way of life, as much as the matter of church order, which had
encouraged many English and Scottish subjects to take up arms against
their king.

Offprint 12 turns from Protestant churchmanship to the problems
facing Catholic clergy in mid-seventeenth-century France. The Counter
Reformation had also placed great stress on improving the religious
understanding of the laity by emphasizing the importance of preaching
and catechizing among the parish clergy, who were required to reside in
their parishes. Their conduct and learning was to be supervised regularly
by the bishops at visitations and special institutions, seminaries, were
created for training the priests. New religious orders, such as the Jesuits,
were also founded to assist in this task. Some of these reforms are very
like those demanded by Protestants, so it is important to remember that
the Sacraments, especially the Eucharist and Confession, remained at the
heart of the Catholic Reformation. The source used here is not contemporary, though it does quote directly from sources of the period; it is
more accurately described as a secondary source, being taken from a very
influential book written by Jean Delumeau in 1970, which has changed
dramatically our understanding of the Counter Reformation within the
Catholic church. The extract discusses the treatment of St John's liturgical cycle, a religious festival which incidentally falls on 24 June, significantly close to the summer solstice.

Exercise   Read Offprint 12 and when you have read the account, read also Briggs,
pp.170–6, and then answer the following questions.

1   What was the main problem facing the Catholic reformers?

2   How did that problem show itself, and what steps did the authorities
take to overcome it?

Discussion I expect that your answer to the first question will include words such as ignorance and superstition, and even paganism. To the second question one might answer that the traditional liturgical calendar of the church had become confused with superstitious practices, such as the wearing of grass belts noted in the extract, which really had nothing to do with religion, but reflected aspects of agrarian folklore. The last part of the question is more complex, the approach of the church was not to ban these festivals but to control them and to 'christianize' them by ensuring that the clergy remained present at the formal part of the festival, and by preventing any opportunity for informal or private celebration alongside the official one. Clearly the church here is meeting traditional culture and working with it to some degree. At this point it is important to avoid being over schematic in how we see religion; in a largely non-literate society ritual and liturgy, which might appear superstitious to our modern eyes, acquired an authentic religious purpose and it would be anachronistic of us to dismiss traditional religious forms too readily as elements of cultural folklore. In this respect the French pastoral practice of the seventeenth century may have been more subtle in its analysis of tradition than the interpretation of some more recent historians.

How do you think that the approach of the French bishops expressed here compares to the ministry of Baxter in England? The answer is not obvious, but it is implied in Baxter's account that he was unsympathetic to the traditional pastimes of the people in his charge; for example, contrast his account of Sunday activities with the sort of events which took place on St John's eve.

I hope that from these two short pieces you have understood that the approach to reform could be very different in Protestant and Catholic countries, the former trying to bring about an intellectual reform through preaching which would eventually reform the lives of the people, the latter attempting to christianize traditional culture and to bring about a reform in the lives of the people through the use of the confessional as well as the pulpit. In broad terms it could be said that the former sought to overthrow popular culture and the second to absorb it; each, however, tried to overcome it.

Between these two polarities were many intermediate points, and it would be quite wrong to see either tradition as monolithic. We have already briefly discussed the different sects which emerged in England during the 1640s and 1650s, we now need to consider the new tradition which emerged within the French church from 1640, and which took its name from Cornelius Jansen, bishop of Ypres in the Spanish Netherlands. Jansen's massive study, the *Augustinus*, was published posthumously in 1640 and became the source text for the new ideas.

Exercise Read Briggs, pp.176–84 part of which you have already referred to in Unit 5. This is a densely packed treatment of a complex issue, so you will need to take notes carefully.

As you go through the passage consider the following questions:

1 How did the Jansenists' dispute differ from previous disputes in the church?

2 What was its intellectual impulse and what did it have in common with Protestantism?

3 What were the consequences of this attitude in the daily lives of its followers? Can you recall any similar responses in Britain?

4 And finally, how attractive was Jansenism to different groups in society?

Discussion 1 Briggs suggests that the earlier disputes were more about ecclesiastical organization, such as the extent to which the French church could act independently of the pope on issues of appointments etc. Jansenism represented a fundamental theological shift which had important consequences in the area of individual spirituality and morality.

2 The Jansenists looked to the Primitive Church of the time of the Apostles and the early Fathers of the first four centuries AD, and also to St Augustine, from which they developed a predestinarian theology which had a lot in common with Calvinism and which took a pessimistic view of human nature.

3 This led to a moral rigorism, not because salvation could be achieved through such behaviour but because that behaviour acted as a witness to one's salvation among the elect, or company of saints. Thus good works became a sign of, rather than the means to, salvation. Failure to demonstrate them raised doubts about one's own election. Consider this in the context of Baxter's description of his congregation.

4 Briggs rightly suggests that Jansenism was a harshly logical creed, and the modern mind might well ask of it, and indeed of Calvinism, why such apparently antipathetic systems of belief, were so popular. Briggs suggests that part of its appeal was in the fact that it became the focus for a range of dissatisfactions against the clergy, and that it drew great strength from the unpopularity of the Jesuits, the religious order in the forefront of the Counter Reformation. Members of the order were powerful at court and made no bones about their aims to dominate the church, not only in France but throughout the Christian world. Their approach was diametrically opposed to that of the Jansenists, in that they sought to make Christianity not separate from the world, but adapted to it and would have been sympathetic to the pastoral style already noted in our discussion of the St John Fires. As such the Jesuits developed a moral teaching which seemed to take a generous view of human frailty, and a theological standpoint which placed great emphasis on pious practices. The trouble was that, although the Jesuits might be generous to the individual in the confessional, they were ruthless exploiters of power in the public sphere, recognizing the need for powerful patrons. This laid them open to charges of cynicism, especially when their moral teaching cast a blind eye on the sins of the mighty (see Briggs p.179).

This is made very clear in *Anthology* II.10. At the time of publication, Antoine Arnauld, the leading Jansenist in France, was facing censure by his colleagues in the theological faculty at the Sorbonne in Paris, following papal condemnation two years previously of five propositions published in the *Augustinus*.

Pascal had come into contact with Jansenism in 1646 when he was 23, and in 1652 his sister had become a nun in the convent at Port Royal, the intellectual power house of the movement. Pascal had acquired a high reputation as a scientist and mathematician in France and used that reputation to pour scorn on the enemies of Jansenism, the Jesuits. This he did in a series of short pamphlets, published between January 1656 and March 1657, which he cast in the form of reports, written by a puzzled bystander to a friend in the country, of the disputes which had been taking place at the Sorbonne. The effect of this is intentionally ironic and exaggerated, at least in the first eleven letters where the comedy of the absurd is never far from the surface. The source therefore is typical of many which historians of religion have to use, in that it derives directly from a bitter controversy. As such it is valuable not so much for the accuracy of its detail, but for what it reveals about the depth of feeling that existed between rival groups. Therefore the tone of the extract is as important as its content. Of course not all controversial writing achieved the literary merit of the *Provincial Letters*, nor their fame (within a year of the publication of the final letter they had been translated and published in England). *Anthology*, II.10 is concerned with the central question concerning what is necessary if one wishes to get to paradise. The learned father in the passage represents the approach of the Jesuits, and he is asked a series of questions, couched in a deceptively simple fashion, by a devout layman.

Exercise   Read *Anthology*, II.10 and try to describe the sort of religion the Jesuit is advocating?

Discussion   This is straightforward enough, it is one which relied on a series of outward devotional practices, such as that of wearing beads to the Virgin. At one level this practice may have been related to the form of prayers to Mary known as the Rosary and still said by Catholics today. At another level, however, such beads may have appeared as a sort of lucky charm bracelet and not very far removed from the sort of superstition which we saw associated with the fires of St John.

Briggs (pp.170–3) suggests that there was a fine line between superstition and devotion in traditional religion, and it is clear from *Anthology*, II.10 that the layman is sceptical about the efficacy of that sort of piety, note the comment at the end. The main objection of the Jansenists therefore was that a religion of this sort would not assist humanity to achieve its divine purpose, but their concern went further than that. *Anthology*, II.10 states that the practices allegedly advocated by the Jesuits would lull sinners into a false sense of security and keep them in their evil ways; and that religion would not be accompanied by that godly conversion of life style which was at the heart of reformed piety at this time, whether Catholic or Protestant. It was precisely that sort of conversion which caused Baxter such pleasure in his ministry at Kidderminster. However, *Anthology*, II.10 is a work of satirical controversy, in which Pascal ridicules his opponents by citing extreme examples. It was not intended to be perfectly fair, so, before you leave the extract you might like to find that part of the dialogue where the Jesuit also mentions the importance of leading a good life.

The *Letters* did not succeed in getting Arnauld re-instated to his post, but their effect was such that in 1657 the Assembly of the Clergy condemned the casuistical style of the Jesuits and the Jansenist position began to have an increasing basis of support among the clergy, even with a few of the bishops. Although they were discriminated against, and never received anything but opposition from the king, the Jansenists were not openly persecuted after the late 1660s until a fresh crisis occurred in the first decade of the eighteenth century. As a group within the broader church in later seventeenth-century France, but at odds with its leadership, their position looked similar to that of the Puritans in early seventeenth-century England, and that similarity appears more marked when one considers that each held to an Augustinian doctrine of Grace, with its strong emphasis on moral reform. In a course of this sort these parallels are important, for they remind us that history should not be written from a too narrowly national or denominational base.

Whilst it is important to point out those features which cut across the great theological divide between Protestants and Catholics, it would be wrong to leave the subject without considering how the position of the

Jansenists and the Puritans differed in relation to their opponents. This is quite difficult, the first point one might consider, that each of them felt excluded from power within the church, only serves to re-inforce the parallels, but there are two significant differences. The first is an institutional one, in France the Jansenists represented a new reforming tradition against an established system, whereas in England the Puritans appeared as the defenders of the Protestant tradition against an innovating group, the Arminians led by Laud, which had captured control of their church. The second relates to the differences between Protestant and Catholic churchmanship: the way in which the Puritans sought to bring about the moral reform they sought was by preaching, the method used by the Jansenists was more commonly through the use of the confessional and the sacrament of penance.

All the extracts discussed so far relate to the 1640s and 1650s, the most disturbed decades of the century, but they have been chosen to represent aspects of what has been called the 'general crisis' of the period. I hope that I have demonstrated that the issues raised in these texts moved far beyond the immediate circumstances of their writing. The final text to be discussed in this section comes from a generation later and returns us once again to Britain.

Gilbert Burnet was born in Edinburgh in 1643, the son of an Episcopalian father and a Presbyterian mother, with whom he never got on (she claimed that he would be 'a bee-headed fool all his life-time'). He admired the moral seriousness of the Presbyterians and was himself renowned for his lack of humour, but was temperamentally drawn to the less rigid Episcopalian tradition. This was due in part to his admiration for the broad undogmatic churchmanship of the Latitudinarian divines he met on a brief visit to England in 1663, and by a journey to Holland the following year. When he returned to take up a parish at Saltoun in Scotland he berated the recently restored Scottish bishops for their insistence on a rigid uniformity in worship. He was threatened with excommunication but refused to withdraw his accusations and went into a brief period of retirement.

In 1669, through the influence of Charles II's Secretary of State in Scotland, the Duke of Lauderdale, and in recognition of his intellectual gifts, he was appointed Professor of Divinity at Glasgow University, undertaking a wholesale reform of the syllabus. Burnet dabbled in Scottish politics in the 1670s and also played a prominent part in the negotiations during the Exclusion Crisis in England, when certain sectors of Protestant opinion sought to debar James, Duke of York, from the succession on account of his Catholicism. Such was his reputation that Burnet was privy to both sides in the dispute, but by then he was best known as a historian, publishing a two-volume *History of the Reformation of the Church of England.*

He played a prominent role on behalf of William and Mary in 1688–9, and was appointed bishop of Salisbury in 1690, a post he held until his death in 1715. His career is therefore a useful example of how, in the later seventeenth century, able individuals could move between English and Scottish ecclesiastical politics. You may recall that those who did so early in the century did so as refugees. Burnet took his duties seriously, and *Anthology,* II.11 gives an account of his actions in that regard, and also describes the duties of a bishop.

Figure 15
Bishop Gilbert Burnet,
after John Riley
c.*1689–91, oil on*
canvas, 74.3 x 62.9 cm.
By courtesy of the National
Portrait Gallery, London.

Exercise   Read *Anthology*, II.11 and draw up a list of the duties of a bishop.

Discussion   My list includes regular theological discussion with the clergy of the diocese (which, on reflection, he thought ineffective), preaching and confirmation, and the examination of ordinands intending to become parish clergy. You might also have included instructing the young, which was part of the confirmation process, and which Burnet also encouraged by the establishment of a school in his cathedral city, and the encouragement of the parochial clergy, often through practical assistance. It is not surprising to find confirmation and ordination in this list, as these were responsibilities particular to bishops, but Burnet does suggest that he was more scrupulous than others in these respects. Consider for example how he makes a point of stressing his personal interest in the examination of prospective clergy, or his description of how he came to devise a more effective method of confirmation in the light of his early experiences in carrying out that office. He was very concerned that the act of confirmation should be the considered choice of an adult Christian rather than be seen as some sort of spiritual rite of passage which naturally followed once the individual reached a certain age.

Throughout the passage there is expressed a concern for the formation of a well-informed Christian laity, led by a conscientious clergy taking special care in the catechizing of the people. (Catechisms were question and answer booklets (usually fairly short, though more detailed versions did exist) which could be used for regular repetition, especially among the young, as a means of instilling in the people the basic tenets of their faith.) This activity, as a prelude to confirmation, he saw as the most effective way of 'reviving Christianity'.

Burnet's high standards meant that he was well aware of the difficulties facing him. He was disappointed with the low level of knowledge of the scriptures exhibited by the ordinands, most of whom were graduates however! He was also uneasy about the casual way that prospective clergy were able to acquire testimonials from well-placed friends about their morals, and he was saddened by the fact that most of the clergy under his charge did not share his desire for toleration. Thus the passage tells not only about the aspirations of a conscientious, reforming, pastoral bishop at the end of the seventeenth century, but it also illustrates the problems he faced in meeting those aspirations.

Now read Briggs, pp.161–70 which describes the difficulties facing reform in the French church, and some of the ways in which they were overcome. You will note of course that the Catholic church had different institutions, such as religious orders, through which it could introduce reform or tackle special problems, but I hope that you will also note the concern expressed for education of the laity, and the increasing desire as the century wore on to have a more consistent form of training for the clergy, including diocesan conferences. The French church, too, wanted a laity versed in the basic beliefs of Christianity, and a clergy well able to teach the same and to provide their congregations with a good pastoral standard of care. In both traditions, by the end of the century, the authorities assumed that Christian teaching would also bring with it Christian and charitable living, and it was to this end that their efforts were directed.

The extracts we have just considered were drawn from both the Catholic and Protestant traditions, and within each we have looked at material which represented the views of those in authority in the churches, and documents which emanated from sources which were anti-establishment or, in Richard Baxter's case, held an ambivalent attitude towards it. Although considerable differences existed on questions of doctrine and over church discipline and worship, all the extracts reveal a concern with the need for a more educated understanding of Christianity, usually requiring a rudimentary level of literacy, and for a more disciplined approach to moral issues. This can be seen as the emergence of a practical and pastoral Christianity, more eirenic, or in our terms ecumenical, in fashion than that form of Christianity which was characterized by those rigorous doctrinal disputes which were rife at the start of our period. This was an important shift in emphasis, and one which had far-reaching consequences, but it is important to remember that it represented aspiration rather than reality. As *Anthology*, II.11 suggests, strong distrust of differing religious traditions was a more commonly held view than Burnet wished for (see also Fig. 17). It is now time to turn to consider the way in which states tried to address the problem of variety in religion during the latter half of the century.

Religious differences after 1660

England and Wales

We have seen that both Baxter and Burnet wrote favourably of toleration, but we have also seen that, in the England of Charles II, Baxter found himself in prison. The return of the Anglican church in 1660 after the upheavals of mid-century resulted in reaction. Despite the hopes of comprehension within a broadly-based Protestantism that were held by churchmen of many persuasions, and the royal promise of 'liberty to tender consciences' the legislation which followed the restoration of Charles, and which was forced on him, resulted in about 2000 clergy refusing to join the new church. It also placed heavy civil restrictions on dissenters, in addition to making their worship illegal. The new church prided itself on its loyalty to the crown; it looked as if an even stronger bond was being formed between church and state than previously, but this did not account for the character of the king. During his exile in France, Charles had been impressed with what he had seen, and had also been attracted to Catholicism. On a number of occasions the king tried to secure toleration for Catholics and for Protestant dissenters, but on each occasion the strong anti-Catholic stance of parliament, coupled with suspicion of Charles's motives, forced him to withdraw.

The years between 1660 and 1688 have come to be known as the 'period of the great persecution' by historians of Nonconformity, but congregations were able to survive under the patronage of powerful supporters like Lord Wharton, whose house at Woburn became a haven for dissenting ministers, and because many local officials, magistrates, town councillors, and parish officers did not bother to impose the strict letter of the law against their neighbours. Dissent had penetrated all sectors of society to such a degree that, while legislation placed obstructions and hardships in the paths of its followers (John Bunyan's *Pilgrim's Progress* was written in prison), it proved ineffective in eradicating it. Not that all leaders of the Established Church wanted to attack dissent, some had shared pulpits with dissenters during the 1650s and others, whilst rejecting the enthusiasm of groups such as the Quakers, recognized that dissent could be an ally in the battle against the increasing tide of immorality, ignorance and atheism which they saw in other developments during these years.

There is an excellent discussion of this in Coward, pp.457–69, from which you should be able to identify the main trends in religious life at this time. Chief among them was a recognition in many quarters that variety in religion was a fact of life. This was expressed on the Anglican side by the Latitudinarians, and recognized by them and by main-stream Protestants in the practice of Occasional Conformity, whereby dissenters could overcome the civil restrictions imposed on them, for example their inability to hold civic office, by receiving the Anglican communion once a year. The High Church party within Anglicanism resisted these trends (the crisis which the Occasional Conformity Act provoked in 1702 is discussed in Coward, pp.404–8), but the Act of Toleration of 1689 recognized the rights of all Protestant congregations to freedom of worship.

One of the influential thinkers who prepared the way for toleration was the philosopher John Locke. Read *Anthology*, II.12 and you will see from what Locke has written that his conclusion is partly conditioned by the way he defines the role of the state, which he limits to the civil sphere, defending the person, property, and material well being of its citizens, but his argument is also based on how he views religion.

Locke clearly states that religion is a matter of belief, in which individual conscience has primacy. The civil powers cannot force people to change their minds against the dictates of conscience, therefore the attempt to impose outward uniformity is doomed to failure. So long as particular beliefs do not threaten the security of the state or the safety of its inhabitants they can, and indeed should be tolerated. This is an important rider, which helps to explain why Catholics continued to be excluded from the Toleration Act. It also reflects Locke's view that religion, properly understood, leads to the 'regulating of men's lives, according to the rules of virtue and piety', thus toleration of such religion should be no problem for the magistrate. Of course, in the world of practical politics, things were more complicated, but in drawing this connection between understanding and behaviour Locke was making the same sort of point, in a different context and with different implications, that has emerged from our discussion of Baxter, Pascal, and Burnet. Locke's letter was very influential among the intelligentsia, and it was an Anglican bishop, Benjamin Hoadley, who declared in 1717 that Christ 'left behind him no visible human authority ... no judges over the consciences or religion of his people' (quoted in Coward, p.463). Put as boldly as that it was an extreme position and led to conflict in the church, but it reflected an increasingly accepted view in educated circles and is one that would have been incomprehensible to Hoadley's predecessors a century earlier.

Figure 16
John Locke,
by Michael Dahl, c.1696,
oil on canvas, 74.9 x 61 cm.
By courtesy of the National
Portrait Gallery, London.

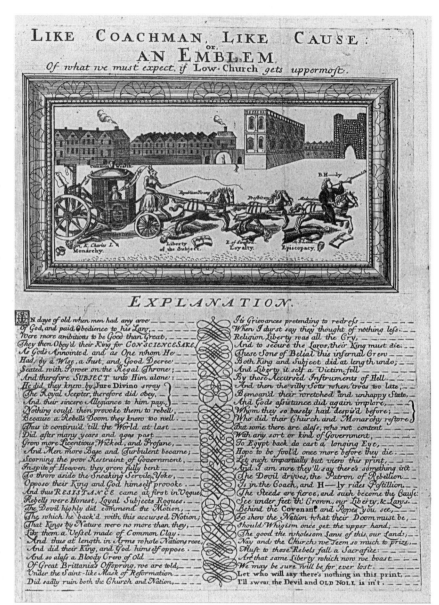

France

Hoadley of course did not intend Catholics to share in this toleration and we should now look to see what was happening in Louis XIV's France. The absolutist policies of Louis's government were not sympathetic to the notion that dissenting groups should be tolerated within the kingdom, and increasing pressures were put on the Huguenots as the reign progressed. Eventually, in 1685, after a number of Protestants had been forced or bribed to abandon their religion, the king thought his position strong enough to revoke the Edict of Nantes.

Although popular with French Catholics the effects of this action were the opposite of those intended. The revocation of the Edict of Nantes arrested the steady drift of Huguenots into the Catholic church and turned them into an underground church which was organized enough to mount a revolt against the crown in 1702 in the region of the Cévennes. It also hastened the emigration of many skilled urban craftsmen, who took the story of their cruel treatment to their new countries. Furthermore, it confirmed the suspicions which Protestant Europe had over French intentions, and even in Catholic Europe it left both pope and emperor unimpressed. Where it did achieve conversions it gave the church pastoral problems at the parochial level which it never really solved. The Huguenots were not the only enemies, however, and the issue of the Jansenists raised its head again early in the 1700s. Details of this crisis are dealt with in Briggs (pp.182–4) and you should read this now.

From this we can see that the Jansenist quarrel had reached international proportions, the conflict with the Jesuits involving both their work in the missions of the Far East and intrigue in the papal court at Rome. For this, and other reasons (remember the French king claimed no doctrinal authority in the church), Louis sought a papal condemnation along the lines of that of 1653. Jansenist activity had moved on since that time, however, and their views had been publicized in a wide range of biblical commentaries and other types of pastoral writings, so that their influence was not confined to France. One of these books, *Moral Reflections on the New Testament*, published by Pasquier Quesnel in 1703, gained a wide circulation, and when the papal condemnation of 1705 seemed to have little effect in bringing the Jansenists to book, Louis sought a further condemnation in the form of a Papal Bull attacking that work in particular. The result was the Bull *Unigenitus*, published in 1713 and condemning 101 propositions in Quesnel's book; that number was selected because the Jesuits claimed that there were over one hundred errors in Quesnel's book.

Important central doctrines of the Jansenists were singled out for condemnation, such as the right of the laity to have free access to the scriptures and their right to participate in the sacraments, as well as the theological point about predestination which we have discussed earlier in the unit. The picture that emerges from the Bull is of an authoritarian institution where access to the mysteries of religion was restricted to the few and where it was the role of the masses to offer unquestioning obedience in the name of peace and order. *Unigenitus* represents the climax of absolutist ambition in religion, but also demonstrates its weakness. Publication of the Bull split the French church. Many clergy and laity identified their own spirituality with that which had been condemned, even though they had never thought of themselves as Jansenists, and some bishops refused to act on it against individuals or groups. In addition the Jansenists received support from local notables in the *parlements*, and they were to retain a place in French Catholicism throughout the eighteenth century.

By the end of our period, therefore, it seems that it was impossible, even with all the force that the French state and church could muster, to impose a uniformity of religion on the people. Elsewhere the need for uniformity itself was being questioned. This was very different from the beginning of the period, when religion was seen to consist largely in the public sphere of worship, and when almost all shades of theological opinion subscribed to the idea that the state should have alongside it an established religion which excluded all other forms of worship. What was witnessed in the period we are studying was an interiorization of religion, as far as individual belief was concerned, with an accompanying stress on a level of literacy which enabled a greater degree of understanding, and a disciplined and regular life style which bore witness to the strength of those beliefs. These are matters which arise in your units on literacy (Unit 6) and on the family (Unit 10) also, and can therefore be seen as part of a wider intellectual and cultural change. Of course, even at the end of the period, High Church Anglicans still held to a strong identification of church and state, whilst the Jesuits in France preached a religion of pious works as well as moral seriousness, but the terms on which the debate took place had shifted dramatically.

Scottish Protestants and Irish Catholics

Before leaving this discussion of religion in the years after 1660 it is important to consider events in Scotland and Ireland. When Charles returned as king of England he also returned as king of Scotland and in 1661 episcopacy was restored to the Church of Ireland. The eclipse of Presbyterianism was not so easily achieved, however, and, though the General Assembly remained suppressed, kirk sessions and local presbyteries continued to exercise local ecclesiastical jurisdiction whilst the Scots were also allowed to keep their traditional order of service. Nevertheless prominent opponents of the Restoration such as Archibald Johnston of Warriston, clerk of the General Assembly in 1638 and author of the National Covenant, were executed. The experiment of episcopacy alongside presbytery was short lived when the rights of patrons, rather than those of congregations, to appoint ministers were restored. As a result hundreds of Puritan clergy, like their English counterparts, resigned their benefices rather than remain within the church, and many of them, especially in the south west of the country, took to holding open air conventicles in the hills.

Troops were sent to put down these meetings and relations between the Presbyterian 'Covenanters' and the Episcopalians deteriorated until, in 1679, open rebellion broke out following the murder, by 'distracted covenanters', of Archbishop John Sharp of St Andrews, one of those who had invited Charles to return in 1660.

The Presbyterians were alarmed at the prospect of the king's brother, the Catholic James, succeeding to the throne, and the 1680s were marked by sporadic violence and persecution known as 'the killing time' which left 'an indelible mark on the soul of Scotland'. About 100 individuals were executed in these years, mostly summarily in the field, and it was the brutality of such circumstances rather than the extent of the repression which earned the title 'killing time'. The reign of James brought concessions to the Catholics in Scotland, but the collapse of his rule was also a calamity for the Episcopalians in Scotland. The Scottish bishops refused to acknowledge William and Mary as sovereigns and stayed away from the parliament which, in 1690, established Presbyterianism as the national church. Thereafter the bishops were inextricably associated with Jacobitism, and thereby with treason, in the minds of their opponents. The triumphant Presbyterian church was not united, however, and the more Puritan elements, who had grown up in the traditional covenanting tradition, saw the terms of the 1690 settlement as betraying that tradition. Furthermore, early in the eighteenth century, the church was split by the emergence of rationalist tendencies within the church, similar to those of the Latitudinarians in England, which were later to lead to secession.

The Restoration of the Stuarts created a division within Irish Catholicism between those who were loyal to the crown and those who were loyal to the papacy. What this meant in effect can be illustrated by the careers of two successive primates of Ireland, Edmund O'Reilly and Oliver Plunkett. O'Reilly became archbishop of Armagh in 1657 and sought to retain the Catholic faith of his people by looking to the traditions of the Gaelic church and by sustaining the pastoral structures of the church come what may. He was opposed by some of the religious orders, notably the Franciscans, who had been influenced by Jansenism and sought a more 'reformed' form of Catholicism, but skilful manipulation of the political processes prevented serious division within the Catholic clergy.

O'Reilly's successor, Oliver Plunkett looked not to native but to European traditions to sustain the church he led from 1669. He sought to bring the Counter Reformation to Ireland from the top down and soon ran into trouble when he sought to appoint Patrick Tyrell as bishop of Clogher over a Gaelic Irish candidate, Phelim O'Neill, a member of a leading Ulster Gaelic family. By the 1670s the Irish church had split into three factions; pro-Jesuit like Plunkett, pro-Jansenist, like the Franciscans, and Gaelic Irish, who were especially strong in Ulster, which included Plunkett's own see of Armagh. Plunkett was a sincere man, and one of great energy. Within six weeks of arriving in the country in 1670 he had held two synods of the clergy, performed two ordinations, and confirmed over 10,000 people, but his determination to restore order on his church made him enemies, especially among the Franciscans whose mission in Ireland he attempted to divide. When that church got embroiled in English politics through the ambivalent attitude of the Stuarts to Catholicism and the traditional suspicion of Irish Catholics among English Protestants, then the archbishop's position became vulnerable. When the Popish Plot broke out in England Plunkett was implicated, partly on the testimony of some Franciscans, and was executed for treason in 1681 without a shred of substantive evidence against him. His fate reflected the strains within Irish Catholicism caused by the question of loyalty to the Stuarts on the one hand, and by the difficulties attendant on bringing the traditional religion of the native population into line with the aspirations of the Counter Reformation on the other.

In this respect the history of religion in both Scotland and Ireland in these years confirms some of the points we have made earlier in our more detailed treatment of France and England.

Religion and morality

We have noted the high value given to uniformity at the beginning of the period and stressed the importance which reformers generally attached to morality as the seventeenth century progressed. Before we leave this unit we should consider what formal instruments were adopted by the church to control these matters. Of course the Catholic church could use the confessional, which was private and confidential and so leaves no records. Historians have to use handbooks of advice written for confessors to try to recover this activity, and we do not have space to consider them here. The Catholic church, like other episcopal churches, also had a system of ecclesiastical courts with its own code of law, Canon Law, and these were used to supplement discipline or to impose it when necessary in the public sphere. The English church had also retained these courts at the Reformation and *Anthology*, II.13 contains an extract from the register of such a court which gives some idea of the business before it at the beginning of the period. This court covered the parish of Stratford-upon-Avon and is peculiar in that it was presided over by the vicar. More usually the courts were organized at diocesan level, and chaired by the bishop or his official, or covered a group of parishes, often in excess of a hundred, which were administered by an archdeacon. The relationship between judge and judged was usually more distant than in our extract, but the type of business dealt with is representative. The cases are those which came to court on 28 May 1622.

Exercise   1   Look at the offences listed in *Anthology*, II.13 and decide which of these were (a) 'moral' and (b) 'ecclesiastical'?

2   How popular do you think the courts may have been, enquiring so closely into people's lives, especially if the officials were more distant figures than the vicar?

Discussion   1 (a) Among the moral offences you will have included 'incontinence' (which we would call fornication), adultery, and slander, where Alice Brunt's good name was besmirched, and you might include 'swearing', though this might also have been ecclesiastical, in that in might have involved blasphemy.

(b)   The ecclesiastical offences include profaning the sabbath by pursuing hobbies and playing traditional games, not going to catechism, not receiving communion, and not attending church. These sort of misdemeanours made up the day-to-day business of the courts.

2   You may have noted that a number of defendants did not appear, no reason is given here but the generally low esteem in which these courts were held meant that many were not minded to attend. This omission incurred excommunication, the chief penalty of the court, an inconvenience which might prevent you having a Christian burial and put other social obstacles in your path; note here, for example, that Thomas Woodward is cited for keeping company with an excommunicate person. Most commonly, though, excommunication would require you either publicly to confess your offence or pay a small fine in commutation of it. Beyond that the exercise of

discipline in this way was an irritant and intrusion, especially when the courts became associated, as they did under Laud, with the enforcement of a particular brand of churchmanship. They were one of the chief objects of attack by the Puritans, who sought a more congregational form of discipline. The church courts did not really regain their disciplinary function over the laity after the civil wars, though they continued to carry out useful administrative tasks, and also acted as a civil court in matters of defamation, marriage and inheritance.

The more localized discipline sought by the Puritans was achieved in Scotland through the kirk sessions, where ministers and leading laymen sat together to administer the moral law. Mitchison and Leneman (1989) has considered the work of these courts. Offprint 13 shows that the kirk sessions in Scotland held on to their disciplinary powers for longer than the English ecclesiastical courts, and that the way in which they conducted their business could be even more intrusive, as the examinations of unmarried women suspected of being pregnant demonstrate. This makes the point that it was not the fact of moral discipline which created opposition to the ecclesiastical courts, but the fact that it was imposed from above by a hierarchical institution, which seemed to be concerned as much with profiting from the petty offences of the people through the imposition of fees and fines as with the reformation of society. This returns us to the question with which we started this unit, where exactly did contemporaries consider that authority in matters of religion was vested? It seems a good point at which to end also.

References

Mitchison, R. and Leneman, L. (1989), *Sexuality and Social Control, Scotland 1660–1780,* Oxford University Press, Oxford.

Russell, C. (1990), *The Causes of the English Civil War,* Clarendon Press, Oxford.

Unit 8
Regional, provincial and local government 1620–1720

Prepared for the course team by Bill Sheils

Contents

Study timetable

Weeks of study	Texts	Video	AC	Set books
2	*Anthology*, II.15–24; Offprints 13, 14	Video 8	AC2, section 4	Coward, Briggs

Objectives
In the course of this unit we will attempt to assess the relationship between central government and the regions and localities over which central government claimed to govern We will also consider sources of both conflict and mutual advantage in the relationship.

Introduction

Before starting work on this unit, it will be useful to refer to the points made in Unit 1, which deals with the institutions of the state, where you learned about the taxation required to maintain the force that was necessary to protect the population against aggressors. This was a central function of the early modern state, but government also had responsibilities to sustain the internal peace of the kingdom so that its citizens could go about their lawful business without 'let or hindrance', as contemporary legal documents expressed it. To assist in the maintenance of that peace governments had also begun to raise taxes for what we might today consider social purposes; much of this taxation, like the English poor law, was raised and spent locally.

In order to maintain law and order in the realm the system of justice and administration were inter-connected. In addition, in France especially, there were significant institutional differences between the provinces, as for example between the *pays d'état*, such as Languedoc,

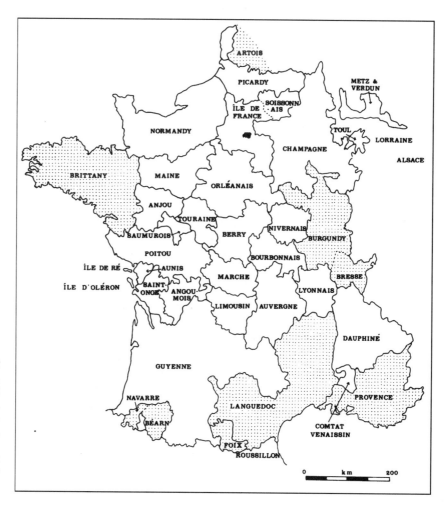

Figure 18
The provinces of France, *reproduced from Richard Bonney,* Society and Government in France under Richelieu and Mazarin 1624–1661, *1988, Macmillan. The* pays d'état *are stippled in a darker colour (e.g. Brittany).*

where the provincial estates retained the right to vote taxes, and the *pays d'élections*, such as Anjou, which did not have such institutions (see Fig. 18).

In Ireland the religious and linguistic differences, following periods of conquest and plantation, had created a country of widely differing communities in which effective central government, beyond the Pale and the larger towns, was extremely difficult. This was especially so where great families like the O'Neills in Tyrone or the McCarthys in Cork managed to hang on to their estates and call on the support of their kin. Furthermore the principal purpose of government policy in Ireland in the early part of the period was to raise revenue for the crown, money which was often spent not in Ireland but in England. This was hardly likely to ensure the co-operation of the native Irish.

In Scotland also the traditional landowners continued to exercise considerable power in the countryside and the bonds of kin remained strong, it being common to follow 'the Name', MacDonalds in the Highlands and Kers in the borders for example, in both politics and religion. This could lead to local faction; Mitchison (1983, p.15) has characterized the situation pithily when she says that 'the problem of Scottish Government was not legislation but execution'.

In differing degrees that was the crucial problem for all early modern governments, though in England a politically sophisticated gentry class also made legislation itself difficult at times, as in the case of ship money, discussed in Unit 3.

All of these factors amounted to a complicated patchwork of overlapping, and sometimes competing, jurisdictions in each of the countries we are studying. For central government they represented both opportunities and difficulties: they could be played off against each other by a skilful and determined ruler or, if the leaders of regional institutions desired, they could combine and prevaricate to obstruct the wishes of central government. In this context the control of patronage, both formal and informal, was crucial to success, and much of the historiography of the early modern state is focused on how this problem was managed. By the end of this unit I hope that you will have a clearer view of the problems facing governors, and how they overcame them.

We will begin with a general account of the main institutions of regional and local government in France and the British Isles and how they related to each other and to the crown. This general account will consider some incidents in the 1630s, when each government was facing problems in raising finance, and be illustrated by more detailed studies of the activities of a justice of the peace in Restoration England and of the responsibilities of the professional *intendant* in late seventeenth-century France. We will then consider the question of patronage, before turning to examine the ways in which localities sought to protect themselves from outside interference in times of crisis. The problems of coping with the more distant regions will be looked at in the context of the Scottish Highlands in the 1680s and of Béarn from the 1620s, and we will then look specifically at the relationship between towns and central government. Finally, at the end of this unit, we will turn away from the relationship of centre and locality to assess how the local governors of a region sought to keep the peace in the latter part of the period.

Provincial government in England and Wales and France

Before we consider the system of regional government in each country it is important to remember the contrast drawn in Unit 1 between the local administration of England, in the hands of part-time, largely unpaid officials, drawn from the ranks of the local land-holding classes, and that in France, carried out by officials who had purchased their office directly from the crown, or had inherited it. The English and French systems therefore had this fundamental difference, even though the aspirations they held and the problems they encountered often appeared very similar.

Please now read Coward, pp.96–100 and Briggs, pp.118–22.

Exercise   Which of the two systems of local government do you think was best integrated into the customary pattern of local power structures and most likely to reflect traditional social relationships?

Discussion   I would think that the English system was more likely to meet those criteria. The French system, especially in the area of taxation, relied heavily on the sale of offices, and it was partly in response to the corruption which this entailed that the crown established the *intendants* as a 'parallel system of non-venal administrators, with tremendous potential as a tool for centralization' to quote Briggs. Note that the *intendants* were generally barred from acting in their native provinces.

England and Wales

We can now look at England and Wales in more detail. Coward lists the main officers on p.96 indicating that they operated at a variety of levels, of which the county, the parish, and the incorporated town were the most important, and he points out that this system 'involved a wide segment of the local community'. He then goes on to say that, in such circumstances, tension between locality and central government was inevitable, and the previous units have given you plenty of examples of that. Coward may overstate this tension, understandably in the light of subsequent events, and it should also be said that, properly managed, such a system also gave an opportunity for a wide sector of the community (as long as they were male!) to participate in the administration of the state. As well as creating tension therefore, local government could also, with astute leadership, encourage involvement.

Exercise   Based on your reading of Coward, list the county officers and their duties.

Discussion   This will not have been difficult and I expect that you will have included the lords lieutenant and their deputies, the sheriffs, and the justices of the peace. We will consider these in turn, but it is important to mention at this point that each of them derived his office from the crown which, in the formal constitutional sense, had control over the local officials; it appointed them and could dismiss them at will. Indeed in the case of the sheriffs and JPs a fresh commission was issued every year, and sheriffs could not continue in office for more than one year in succession.

The most senior officer was the lord lieutenant, who often had responsibility for more than one county and was usually assisted by deputies. He was almost always a member of the nobility and his chief responsibility was to ensure that the militia was maintained, that freeholders provided arms, and themselves, to defend the realm, and that they were properly trained. The raising of the militia had developed on customary lines, but in the 1620s, the government sought to reorganize the military on more efficient lines and create what it called an 'exact militia'. This was to be done through the lords lieutenant and involved the payment, from the county rates, of professional soldiers, called 'muster masters', to train the locals. The resulting billeting of soldiers on the localities and the extra expense on the rates, led the gentry in several areas to protest about what they saw as infringements of local liberties so that, in the end, the Privy Council was forced to withdraw its more ambitious schemes. The dispute reveals both the strength of local loyalty, and also its narrow geographical focus, for the soldiers being billeted were often from no more than twenty miles away.

Although the lord lieutenant was senior in status, the office of sheriff was of much greater longevity. It had previously represented the pinnacle of local standing for the gentry of a county, but by the seventeenth century had lost much of its earlier importance. Its functions were largely formal and, like most formal responsibilities, had become expensive to the office-holder. It had thus come to be seen as a burden as much as an honour by many of the county gentry, except at election times when the sheriff presided over the county elections and could thereby use his influence in securing the local members of parliament.

The main burden of county government was borne by the JPs whose judicial and administrative activities increased enormously during the period, a fact which in itself expresses both the widening range of activity undertaken by government and the increasing degree of penetration by the centre into the localities. They acted as magistrates in the county courts, or quarter sessions, sitting in judgement on criminal cases and issuing licences for all manner of activities from alehouse keeping to highway maintenance. They also supervised the officials in the lesser jurisdictions, such as parish officers.

Exercise   Read *Anthology*, II.15 which describes the range of activities undertaken by a JP from Essex in the later seventeenth century. (Note that his commission related to the forest at Epping, so his title reflects that situation in that he is referred to as a verderer, but his functions were essentially

Figure 19
Titlepage of A Manuall or Analecta *formerly called The Compleat Justice, 6th edition, 1648. The titlepage of a handbook for justices of the peace, which forms a pictorial eulogy of some of the great names of the common law tradition: Sir Edward Coke, Richard Crompton, Michael Dalton, William Lambarde and Sir Thomas Littleton. Dalton and Lambarde were authors of such handbooks. Copyright © British Museum Dept of Prints and Drawings BMC732 reproduced by permission of the Trustees.*

those of a JP.) Now list some of those responsibilities recorded in his note book. What else does this tell you?

Discussion   First, of course, it was his job to protect the forest wild life, which was the property of the king, and to prosecute poachers. He also kept the peace between the inhabitants of the forest, dealing with accusations of assault or of theft between parties, and sat in judgement between masters and their apprentices, and even between husbands and wives in one case of alleged bigamy! In addition he dealt with petitions for licences, noting one for enclosing a piece of ground at Leyton and another for felling wood at Loughton; issued orders to the constables of the forest for the transport and incarceration of prisoners; and, on the orders of the lord lieutenant, raised a company of militia for a month's training.

The account also tells us that this was a busy life, especially as it was unpaid. Furthermore the magistrate involved, William Holcroft, was not a wealthy man, having relatively recently settled in the area and holding a modest estate. Apart from this source we know very little about him, and this appointment seems to have been the most important office he acquired. The source therefore not only informs us about the range of activities which came before JPs but also reminds us of Coward's point (p.96) about the way in which a wide segment of local society could be involved. Clearly Holcroft thought it his duty to accept these responsibilities and his appointment both expressed and reinforced his standing in the local community.

It was the ambition of almost all men who were of gentry status to be appointed to the bench, and it was important for the more substantial of the landowners to be named one of the quorum, one of whom had to be present before the magistrates could be deemed to be in full session. Therefore, even among the JPs, there were different levels of status which reflected the local hierarchy. In such a system, requiring so much work from unpaid officials, it was essential that the crown was sensitive to local opinion. You have already studied the example of ship money (Unit 3) but it is worth returning to the subject briefly at this point.

Exercise   Turn to the *Anthology* (II.16). Describe the nature of the objections made by a Kent JP, Sir Anthony Weldon in 1637.

Discussion   Kent was, of course, a maritime county and therefore familiar with the tax, and I hope that you have noted that Sir Anthony's objections are concerned with the manner in which it was raised rather than with the underlying principles. Instead of leaving matters to the discretion of the sheriffs and high constables he recommends that traditional levies, the composition for the hundreds (which were groups of neighbouring parishes, usually about 20 in number), and the poor rate for the parishes, should be the measures by which ship money should be assessed. Thus the argument states that the locality will respond more favourably to a tax based on customary levies, than one which was fixed by a few individuals given that authority by the crown. (Note here that Weldon does not suggest that the traditional system is necessarily fairer or more efficient than the new, but 'better any Rule, then the discretion of one man', i.e., customary practices, even when 'partial' themselves, are a defence against arbitrary action.) Weldon's conclusion 'What is imposed by Superiors we take patiently, but if by equals or Inferiors it cannot be so well digested', also signals the difficulties facing central government. It highlights the care which the crown had to exercise in appointing local officials and testifies to the degree of solidarity which regular involvement in local government had created among JPs in Kent and elsewhere, which historians have called the 'county community'.

ie ship money

Charles had tried to circumvent the opposition of the JPs to his measure by giving greater powers to the sheriffs and also, in this case (*Anthology*, II.16), to the High Constables, described as 'mean fellows' by Weldon. Such an attempt to ignore the local social hierarchy, however attractive in theory, had serious practical consequences for the implementation of policy. Although the crown had the formal right of appointment of JPs it was in practice a limited power, as Charles I was to discover. It was no good placing loyal men of low social status on the bench, as he did in several counties during the 1630s, in order to secure unpopular royal policy against the wishes of the more substantial landowners, for such men did not have the local clout to prevail against the wishes of their social superiors. These more substantial gentry saw themselves, quite correctly in view of the experience their families had acquired over the previous century, as the traditional authority in their own 'countries', as they called their counties.

The JPs therefore derived their power as local governors from their standing in their local communities and not from royal favour, and when the crown sought to overturn established local hierarchies, it was likely to suffer a rebuff. Furthermore the power of the more substantial of the JPs as local administrators was enhanced by the experience which many of them gained as central legislators whilst sitting in parliament. Not only did this allow them to see central government at close quarters but it also gave them the opportunity to exchange views and compare experiences which transcended their own localities. Thus through their work as MPs, and through bonds of friendship formed at university and at the Inns of Court, English local governors could develop a sense of national interest based on a cumulative set of local experiences which could provide an alternative sense of national destiny to that which emanated outwards from the centre. In this way the tension was not simply one between the centre and the locality, but was also about differing perceptions of the nation.

It would be wrong to suggest that the crown had no real power against the JPs, and sometimes it could use the lords lieutenant to keep recalcitrant justices in line. There were also the traditional institutions of the church and the law. The crown could usually depend on the bishops to support their policies, and the richer diocesans, such as Winchester or York, held estates, and through those patronage, which compared favourably with those of the wealthier gentry in their locality. Their effectiveness was often limited by their circumstances, however; they were rarely local themselves and so found it difficult to integrate with their social peers; sometimes they were also men of relatively humble origin whose need to advance their families through grants of leases could conflict with established local practice; they usually came to their bishopric late in their careers and so were not likely to be in office in one diocese for more than a few years; finally, and most damagingly, in the early years of the period many of them were, as Arminians, associated with a churchmanship which was not only antipathetic to the gentry but also to many of their parish clergy.

These all represented difficulties in the way of bishops as local agents of central government, but they did have their uses. They could report back to the crown on local affairs and on the reliability of particular individuals, and it is worth reminding ourselves that the Bishop of Durham was not only the leading churchman but also the wealthiest landowner and chief magistrate of that county, hence the title 'Prince-Bishop'. He was, however, the exception.

As for the Law, the Judges of Assize went round on their circuits, which covered groups of counties, checking up on JPs and hearing the more important court cases. They acted as a channel through which orders from the centre could be communicated to the locality and one through which local intelligence could be brought back to the government. Their visits to any one county, however, were brief, only amounting to a matter of weeks in a year so that the information they could glean was necessarily limited.

In addition to these traditional institutions the previous century had seen the secure establishment of two regional councils staffed by lawyers, senior clergy, and leading local landowners, which were directly responsible to the Privy Council: they were the Council of the North based at York, covering Yorkshire and the counties nearest to Scotland, and the Council of the Marches, dealing with Wales and its border counties. These were designed to support central government in difficult border regions where the need for loyalty among the landowning population was paramount. They were abolished in the civil war and not revived at the Restoration, by which time these regions had been more thoroughly integrated into the normal institutions of the state.

France

The French system had emerged in a piece-meal way and large and important provinces, such as Guyenne, Burgundy, Brittany and Provence, had only come under the French monarchy in the fifteenth century. In some respects the problems facing the French crown in these regions were more like those which faced English rulers in Wales and Ireland, overcoming distinct linguistic and cultural traditions for example, than those which the latter confronted in say Lancashire. These French provinces, known as the *pays d'état*, retained their traditional representative institutions, or estates, which, rather like the Irish parliament, retained control over taxation in their province. As such their privileges were viewed as an obstacle to effective central government and in the late 1620s the finance minister, Marillac, sought to establish uniformity throughout the kingdom. He attempted to introduce the system of *élections* (financial courts staffed by officials who had purchased their office from the crown), which existed in the rest of France, to the *pays d'état*. The result shows how compromise was reached in the delicate matters of negotiation between centre and region, for it is uncertain whether the implications of the full-scale adoption of *élections* were really contemplated, representing as they did a major curbing of local autonomy. Instead the province could resist the imposition of *élections* if it raised enough money to compensate the crown for the revenue which the royal financiers anticipated from the sale of offices in the new financial courts. This is exactly what took place in Provence, Languedoc and Burgundy, and it was only in Dauphiné, where faction within the estates prevented united opposition to royal policy, that *élections* were established on a permanent basis. This incident recalls the pattern of relationships described by Briggs (p.97), that 'generally it suited both sides to reach a compromise, so the outcome was a repeated pattern of exaggerated royal demands, followed by threats of resistance and negotiations, ending in substantial modifications to the original proposals'. This sort of 'barter' system, which reconciled the declared and real objectives of government, has to be kept in mind when assessing the relationship between the crown and its more powerful institutional subjects throughout the period.

The officials who served in the *élections*, the *élus*, had purchased their office from the crown, and this serves as an introduction to the institution which underpinned the French administrative system, the *paulette*. This was initiated in the first decade of the seventeenth century as a means whereby office-holders, through an annual payment to the crown out of the profits of their office, could ensure that their descendants would succeed to the position in the event of their death. The security this offered to the office-holder was matched by the regular income that the *paulette* provided for the crown, and in its early years the mutual advantage derived was generally accepted. In fact the system of venality was an effective source of stability, producing local élites with a vested interest in secure central government and has been interpreted by some as one of the main reasons for the end of Wars of the Religion of the sixteenth century. Once the system became established, however, the crown could exploit it to raise even more revenue either by increasing the financial demands on existing officers or by creating new offices. The exigencies of financing wars made this an easy option for the crown and as early as 1625 Richelieu had been warning against essentially short-term advantages.

Notwithstanding such warnings, however, Richelieu presided over the greatest expansion of venal office in French history, and that growth continued after him. Recent estimates suggest that, by 1665, there were at least 50,000 office-holders, with an additional 20,000 tax farmers and 10,000 clerks, amounting to one official for every 200 inhabitants. Despite Louis XIV's attempts in the early years of his reign to reduce the disadvantages associated with the system, most notably the corruption which stemmed from the high price of office, and the restrictions which the system imposed on the king's right to choose his own officers, royal attempts at reform were defeated by the immediate need to raise money for war finance. The unsatisfactory system endured.

Thus local and regional officials in France derived their authority from a very different source from their English and Welsh counterparts and, in some respects, were less easy to remove.

Maintenance of law and order in the provinces rested with the sovereign courts, and in particular the *parlements*, of which there were eight at the start of the period. That at Paris was the most senior, followed by that of Toulouse and those of Grenoble and Bordeaux. More recently *parlements* had also been established at Dijon, Rouen, Aix-en-Provence and Rennes, whilst in the early part of our period *parlements* were set up at Pau in 1620, to oversee the south-west regions, and at Metz in 1633, to deal with recently conquered territories. By 1714 *parlements* had also been established at Douai, Besançon, and Nancy. All of them were modelled on the Paris *parlement* and saw themselves as sovereign courts in their own regions. Their responsibilities were extensive and the following description of the work of the *parlement* at Besançon gives an overview of their activities:

> *Parlement* had jurisdiction over everything to do with fiefs, finance, important police matters, defence of cities, fortifications, the pay and levy of troops, billeting, transportation, and subsistence of soldiers, legal formalization of acquisitions made by religious communities, surveillance of church-connected colleges, hospitals, prisons, and factories, defence of the Catholic religion, punishment of abuses by the spiritual authorities, liberties of the Gallican Church, alleviation of peasant suffering in case of crop failure, price control on bread and other much needed commodities, stocking of markets, observation and reform of local customs, interpretation of regulations, upkeep of cities and public sanitation, surveillance of beggars and vagabonds, recruitment of the militia, award of public works contracts, horse breeding, cadastral surveys, the sol [or sou, i.e. penny], and construction of roads and canals. (Mousnier, 1984, p.260)

In addition one could add the defence of local and provincial privileges and the adaptation of French law to local custom and usage.

As sovereign courts the *parlements* defended the customary constitution of their provinces, but the crown could exercise influence through the office-holders who made up a large part of membership. The interests of office-holders became a central preoccupation, sometimes putting the *parlement* at odds with other sectors of provincial society, such as the nobility, townsmen or peasantry, as we have seen at Bordeaux in 1651. Despite this social limitation, however, the *parlements* were marked by a strong regionalism, borne of their role as the guardians of local rights and privileges, which meant that the different *parlements* rarely united to form a more concerted opposition to royal policy. Toulouse expressed some interest in union with Paris, but in the end the freedom to bargain directly with government and gain local concessions was paramount and nothing came of the plan. The Paris *parlement* had little influence on events in the provinces and almost all local treaties negotiated during the Frondes, for example, were done so independently.

Exercise   In the light of the above comments, look back at the discussion of the magistrates in England and compare their opportunities to extend their interests beyond purely local concerns.

Discussion   I imagine that you have picked out the legislative role of many English magistrates as MPs as a significant difference in this respect. They moved more easily between the centre and the locality than their French counterparts.

We have only briefly set out the administrative structure of France which Bonney, its leading English historian, has described 'as very complex' and defying 'any convenient description in tabular form' (Bonney, 1988, p.83) but I hope that this has signalled to you some of the key features of that structure.

Exercise   Before going any further, and by way of recapitulation, I would like you to itemize those features in the administration of French regional and local government which you consider particularly important.

Discussion   You would probably place the sale of offices first, and then would include the variety of provincial institutions, the presence of a class of office-holders with their own particular agenda in each region, and the apparent lack of opportunity to move easily between provincial and central government in the way that the English gentry could do.

    You may also have included the extent to which central government used local and regional government as a tool of fiscal policy or, using the example of the Besançon *parlement*, noted the all-embracing nature of its responsibilities. Many of these, such as the oversight of the poor, were much the same as those undertaken by English magistrates, but the *parlement* laid more stress on military concerns than was customary in English local institutions.

Although these are important, I would return to the sale of offices and the implications which that had for the efficiency of local administration.

    In attempting to meet that issue a most radical change in regional government was made. The *intendants* had been used in a piece-meal way during the sixteenth century but in 1634 the first step was taken to develop their systematic use when a commission was issued throughout the *pays d'élections* for the reform of the *taille*. The commissioners were appointed for each *généralité* (see Fig.20), the standard administrative unit for taxation purposes, and were given the responsibility to examine charges of corruption against local officials and deal summarily with the more obvious cases of inequity.

Exercise   Read the account in *Anthology*, II.17, and identify the chief source of corruption and the consequences of which the commissioners complain.

Discussion   It is pretty clear that the principal way in which the locals were avoiding the *taille* was through false claims to titles of nobility which granted them exemption from the tax. The commissioners found that the local officials, the *élus*, made no enquiry about the truth of these claims,

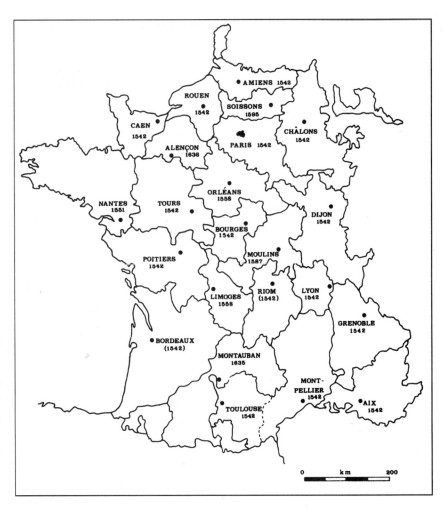

Figure 20
The généralitiés of France
at the time of Richelieu
and Mazarin. *The date
indicated the year in which
the généralitié was established.
Reproduced from Richard
Bonney,* Society and
Government under
Richelieu and Mazarin
1624–1661, *1988,
Macmillan.*

despite the obvious nature of the fraud – a state of affairs which meant that the burden of taxation in the *généralité* fell chiefly on the third estate, the peasantry and artisans. Thus questions of taxation and peace-keeping were inextricably linked, and when the costs of war resulted in increased taxation in 1636–7 a number of peasant risings ensued.

Exercise   Read *Anthology*, II.18 which is an account of a peasant rising in Angoumois. List the demands of the rebels.

Discussion   1   The level of taxation, and in particular the new taxes, was itself a source of grievance, and responsibility for this was placed at the door of the Council and 'the gentlemen of Paris'.

2   Abolition of the new impositions was demanded, for the *taille* and other traditional dues ought to have produced enough income if 'properly spent'.

3   The costs of war were recognized but the peasants insisted that new levies should only be raised after a vote by the Estates-General, a

body which last met in 1614–15 and was not to meet again until the Revolution of 1789.

You may also have noted the appeal to tradition in *Anthology*, II.18, which was also a feature of the ship money complaint. The real point at issue, however, seems to have been the corruption of the officials responsible for collecting the taxes, the *élus* were themselves said to be the richest men in the locality, and yet they paid no tax whatsoever. They also gave exemptions to tenants of their friends, thereby placing the full burden on that part of the community least able to pay. Thus the system impoverished the province and increased the personal wealth of a few office-holding individuals. It was against the background of these sorts of problems that Richelieu sought to extend the role of the *intendants*, and they were given special responsibility to supervise the work of the *élus*. The *intendants* began to fix the levels of the *taille* rather than leaving that to local officials, and they were given an increasing role in the administration of justice. Their workload developed as the century wore on, as can be seen by the annual instructions reproduced in the *Anthology* (II.19) for the year 1680.

Exercise　Read *Anthology*, II.19 and list the main responsibilities of the *intendants*.

Discussion　1　The *intendants* were asked to improve their performance!

2　The *intendants* were to survey the local agriculture and industry and to visit some of the towns in the *élection* to report on the administration of the *taille*.

3　Each *intendant* was asked to check that the tax assessments had been made equitably, and to hear all complaints about unfair treatment by the local officials, suspending the most corrupt of them.

4　Methods to improve the efficiency of collection were to be devised, and reports of the sums raised in the last year sent in.

5　Notification of all those imprisoned for offences to do with the *taille* was required, but the collectors were to be ordered not to impound livestock as this would merely impoverish the peasants and make them even less able to pay in future.

6　The *intendants* were to investigate any problems with the collection of indirect taxes, to attend to the royal will regarding those communities in debt from previous years, and to supervise all matters relating to the coinage.

Two further things of interest emerge from this document, the first from its content and the second from its tone. Clearly the list of tasks implies a high degree of supervision by the *intendants* over the activities of local officials, but the tone also suggests a high degree of supervision over the *intendants* by the centre. Phrases such as 'The King has instructed me to repeat most strongly to you', or 'he will be able to see, from the places and dates at the head of your letters, whether or not you have carried out his orders promptly', smack strongly of big brother. Was this really so?, and who were these men?

A crucial point about the *intendants* is that they were usually outsiders to the *généralité* in which they worked, and so had no vested interest in the locality, and in order to reduce the risk of an *intendant* becoming too involved in the life of the *généralité* they were normally moved to a different post after a few years. Almost as important was the fact that the office could not be purchased, so that, on the one hand, an inefficient *intendant* could easily be dismissed and, on the other, there were no barriers to the promotion of the able. Indeed the office was an important rung on the ladder of promotion within the sovereign courts of justice and most of the *intendants* came from well-established office-holding families. Successful performance of their duties could gain them entrance to the very heart of government (e.g. Michel Le Peletier became director-general of inland and coastal fortifications in 1691 after 15 years as *intendant* in Flanders).

It is clear from the range and importance of the duties entrusted to them that the *intendants* had to be men of some status if they were to carry out their functions effectively, for though small in number (there were never more than fifty) they acted as the eyes and ears of Paris throughout the kingdom. In this way, of course, they had considerable influence, but central government sought to control this by restricting their executive power. They were responsible for the supervision of the local officials, and their information guided central government to important issues of policy, but the execution of that policy was almost always entrusted to the ordinary members of the bureaucracy, the venal office-holders, with the *intendant* reporting on their actions. His job was to observe the local officials, not to replace them. It remains a matter of debate among historians as to how effective these men were in reforming local government and increasing the power of the crown. Their achievements only came slowly, and were most marked in the last 30 years of our period. They were most effective in the *pays d'élections*, and had less success in the *pays d'état* or in the larger cities such as Marseille or Lyon, where the estates and the town councils had a tradition of autonomy and sufficient power to exercise it. Furthermore, their increasing involvement in almost every aspect of royal policy made it harder for them to do everything thoroughly, and they were distinctly overworked. Finally, however hard they worked, they also had to contend with the sheer size of France, and the consequent delays in the passage of information between the localities and Paris.

What can be said for the great majority of them is that, though the work was hard, the rewards for loyalty were significant and examples of corruption among them were relatively rare. The 'honour of service' was a leading motive of all *intendants*, as the career of Nicolas de Basville demonstrates. He was born in 1648 and, after a career in the Paris *parlement*, served successively as *intendant* at Montauban, Pau, and Poitiers until he was named councillor of state and *intendant* for Languedoc in 1685. Languedoc was a province with a strong Huguenot presence, resented by the provincial nobility, and in the aftermath of the Revocation of the Edict of Nantes, Basville arrived in the province at the head of a military force. His brilliance as an administrator made him essential to the crown, and his sympathy for local custom and his humane treatment of opponents, even during the Camisard revolts, made him acceptable to the provincial leaders. Therefore, exceptionally for an *intendant*, he did not leave the province after 1685 until his retirement in 1718, not even for the deaths of his mother in 1705 and his brother in 1709. His son, Urbain-Guillaume, was *intendant* of Rouen from 1704 to 1709, when he was transferred to Guyenne. On his way to Bordeaux he spent three days with his father, whom he had not seen for twelve years, and they spent that time discussing ways of executing orders common to both Guyenne and Languedoc. Thereafter they never saw each other without the official permission of the *controleur général* in Paris. Such dedication was by no means unusual among this class of men.

These rather lengthy discussions of England and Wales and France have provided you with detail for the general suggestions about the differences between the two systems which were noted at the beginning of this unit, and you may wish to remind yourselves of these now and mark those passages in the above account which best illustrate these points.

In addition to these differences we have seen that, in terms of their ambitions for effective local government, the rulers of both countries had a lot in common, even if the means by which they hoped to achieve those ambitions varied. We have also seen that central government in both countries could be obstructed in those ambitions if it did not take account of local custom and social structure. One of the most effective means of bringing the ambitions of central government in line with the aspirations of regional authorities was through the exercise of patronage.

Patronage

It should be clear to you by now that the task of government required considerable political skill in the manipulation of patronage. You will have seen in Unit 2 how the culture of the royal households in both the British Isles and France were based on royal favour or patronage, and that the monarchs sought to increase their influence in these matters as the century progressed. The discussion of the *intendants* above also shows how dependent they were on their ability to satisfy the demands of the crown. Patronage was the oil which kept the wheels of government turning, and in both France and Britain the crown was at the centre of extensive patronage networks, both formal and informal, which provided it with a powerful instrument of government. Mitchison (1983) traces the shift in political culture in Scotland with which this course is concerned. That shift did not take place everywhere, as we shall see below when we consider the Highlands, but wherever possible patronage or persuasion rather than force were the preferred instruments of policy.

At the most important level patronage emanated from the crown, but there were other sources of patronage also: Irish chiefs, Scottish clans, English gentlemen, French nobles, and town governments in all countries had influence over their tenants or their less well-off neighbours. This sort of patronage, or clientage, could create difficulties for government by setting up counter and competing networks to frustrate royal ambitions. Nor was it always easy for the crown to ignore these: as we have seen in the case of ship money, it was one thing to appoint people to carry out policy, it was quite another to ensure that they had the necessary standing to be able to deliver. Patronage was, therefore, constrained by social and political hierarchies, and whilst a few able individuals could overcome these when in pursuit of acceptable policies, if the individual was weak or the policy unpopular the problem could prove insurmountable.

This discussion is very much at the level of generality, but to give point to the analysis it is best to move to the particular and to see the workings of patronage in action. We shall do this by considering how the French government dealt with noble and administrative clienteles in Marseille during the mid-seventeenth century and for this you will need to read Offprint 14. This is a densely argued piece, which addresses an issue at the very heart of early modern government, so we will spend some time on it. To help to take you through this material we will turn to the accompanying audio-cassette (AC2, section 4). Listen to the audio-cassette now.

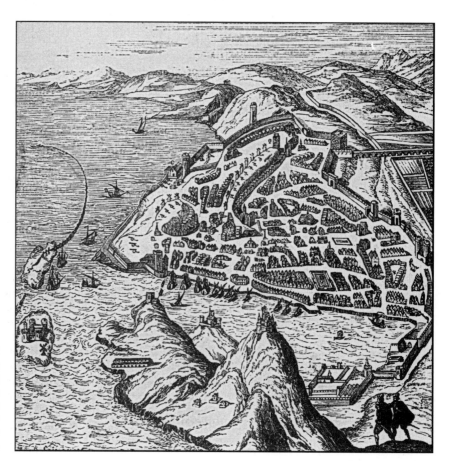

Figure 21
View and plan of Marseille and its harbour in the sixteenth century, from a copper plate in the collection of G. Bruin in 'Théatre des Cités de Monde'. Mary Evans Picture Library.

From this discussion you will realize that patronage relationships helped to determine individual political behaviour in this period, and that they were supplementary to and operated outside of the formal institutional structures we have discussed, though it is important to note that they tried to operate those formal structures to their advantage where possible. It was also the case that these networks functioned at a variety of levels, nationally, regionally and locally, and that their basis could be both personal, around a family like the Valbelles, or institutional, through the *parlement* at Aix. The crucial point was that patronage produced political machines which enabled the patrons to exercise power and to govern. Its management, therefore, was essential to success at every level of politics; the state, the region, the locality, and the town.

Localities and regions

So far in this unit we have described the administrative systems devised for local and regional government, and discussed the importance of the exercise of patronage to the successful operation of those structures. In the course of that discussion some of the problems which faced central government in the localities have been mentioned, but it is now time to switch our focus more directly on to the localities themselves. You will have already considered the debate about 'court' and 'country' in England in the years up to the civil war, and we have already referred incidentally to the fact that JPs often referred to their county as their 'country'. If you have a basic knowledge of French you will also have some idea of the ambiguities which surround the word '*pays*', which expresses more than a geographic location, including in its meaning a variety of institutional, social, and cultural elements distinctive to an area. Clearly there was a strong sense of local and regional identity in early modern Britain and France which, at various times, came into conflict with the state.

Appeals to custom and tradition formed part of this local loyalty in the 1630s, and in Unit 5 you spent some time on the challenges facing central authority in both Britain and France during the 1650s when, after the execution of one king and during the minority of another, both governments were subject to periods of particular stress. Yet that particular unit is entitled 'The return to internal stability' and recounts, after discussion of several risings and revolts, the return of strong central government under an effective monarch. Those risings and revolts were often specific in location but they also involved a variety of religious, constitutional, and social issues of more general application. It is not always possible, of course, to separate these different motives, but in an attempt to assess the political importance of local and regional identity, and the way in which it impacted on the state we will consider three contexts.

First, we will look at a mid-century movement which some historians have seen as an especially important reflection of local loyalties

Secondly, we will turn to those regions at some distance from the centre, and which often had differing linguistic and cultural norms.

Thirdly, we will consider the way in which those most concentrated of local units, the towns, reacted with central government.

The Clubmen

The county associations known as Clubmen were formed during the military phase of the civil war in 1645. By that date several localities had suffered from the presence of soldiers. In Wiltshire, for example, law and order had been steadily eroded during 1643 and 1644 and confrontations between peasantry and soldiery had resulted in a series of violent episodes and plundering of country houses; neither royalist nor parliamentary commissioners, each of whom were nominally in control of different parts of the county, could suppress this activity, and all attempts to raise the assessments were abandoned. The breakdown of the peace negotiations at Uxbridge and the discussions held with the Scots about the Presbyterian Directory of Public Worship early in 1645 helped to bring the clergy and the gentry into what had previously been peasant associations, involving yeomen and farmers, which had organized themselves to defend their own and neighbouring villages from plunder by soldiers or others.

The gentry were able to dominate the movements, by getting themselves proclaimed 'directors' at mass meetings, and they broadened the political objectives, demanding a national settlement to the war. Essentially however, they were local defence committees, as *Anthology* (II.20) suggests, which proclaimed themselves neutral from either army. It is no surprise to find that such associations emerged in several counties in the west and the midlands, where military activity had been fiercest. Although they shared common general aspirations, however, the county remained the essential organizational base and local circumstances and prejudices figure prominently in the papers surviving from each area.

Their petitions reveal little constitutional understanding and their localism was expressed chiefly in an adherence to custom and a determination to restore traditional structures, the abandonment of which they saw as a chief cause of the war. In that respect they reflected the views of many contemporaries, but though the movement revealed a spirit of independence among the peasantry and testified to the integrity of county ideals throughout the war, the associations were responding to the breakdown of central authority and demanding a say in its restoration rather than advocating a more localized structure.

Like the Ormée in Bordeaux, which you studied in Unit 3, the Clubmen represented an attempt to protect local interests. They did so by an appeal to tradition, and the Ormée by a call for radical change but each, in their attempt to give substance to their community of interest by joining in associations (not unlike the covenanting tradition we noted in Scotland in Unit 7), gave tangible expression to the importance of localism as a factor in political life of the period. That importance was, in the context of the mid-century upheavals, a limited one however, and in the end each movement failed to transcend the circumstances of time and place which had brought it into being. For the enduring strength of regional traditions we need to look elsewhere, and should now turn our attention to the more distant regions of the state.

Distant regions

The importance of the Irish rebellion of 1641 as a catalyst to the outbreak of civil war in Britain has already been discussed in Unit 3 and the associated audio exercise, and you may care to remind yourself of that discussion and the importance of the Ulster gentry, the leaders of local traditional society, in those events. The issues discussed there are also important for the debate we are currently engaged on, but rather than repeat points made there we will move forward a few decades and look at another region of Britain, the Scottish Highlands. In the later seventeenth century they also illustrated the difficulties facing central government in far flung regions with very different cultural traditions. Highland culture was still aural, based on music and song, in which women were as likely as men to figure in the role of guardian of the traditions. Those traditions, however, were based on the clan system where the chiefs retained great sway over the lives of their tenants and families in a wretchedly poor countryside. The Glencairn Rising against Cromwell (see Unit 5), revealed the limits of rebellion against a strong central power prepared to meet the threat of opposition with brutal destruction. As suggested in Unit 5, that rising 'sunk back whence it had come, into the turbulent waters of Highland lawlessness'. The most recent study of the Highlands in this period (Macinnes, 1986) suggests that its reputation for lawlessness has been exaggerated, but even its author is forced to describe local government in the region as a matter of 'hereditary private enterprise', a phrase which is not indicative of much sense of purposeful direction.

During the 1670s Highland society was immersed in a clan war between the Campbells and MacLeans and the government was losing what little control it had, but the exile of Archibald Campbell, Earl of Argyll, in 1681 gave the crown the opportunity to attempt a new policy towards the region. This it did by setting up a Commission of Highland Justiciary which removed the administration of justice from the Campbells and their supporters, and placed it in the hands, not of magnates, but of 75 lairds and chiefs. It survived for little over two years, and marked a change in government policy towards the region which, prior to that time, consisted of neglect interrupted by short periods of repression. Its success was patchy and, as *Anthology*, II.22 illustrates, much still remained to be done when the Commission was disbanded later that year.

Exercise   Turn to *Anthology*, II.22 and read the report of the commissioners. How do the commissioners feel about the task which they have been allotted?

Discussion   Like all such groups they are keen to give a glowing account of their achievement over the previous two years, 'by their indefatigable pains the frequent thieving and robbing … is now so happily suppressed', but they then reveal their self interest in asking to be released in order to return to 'their own necessary affairs', which they have been forced to neglect to their cost.

This illustrates the problems of having amateur officials who did not have the personal resources, as had the magnates, to bear the opportunity costs of office and who could not see how, because of the nature of the clan system, government service in the local arena would increase their social or political standing. In this respect the Highlands were very different from, say, Essex where minor gentry happily took on a role in local government.

Exercise   Look now at the recommendations made by the commissioners and list these in the order they are placed on the report.

Discussion   The first proposal is for the placing of a garrison at Inverlochy (a suggestion which is itself testimony to the lawless nature of the area and the limitations imposed upon a central government trying to use local structures to maintain peace in a region).

The second article refers to the local systems of lordship, and requires that the nobility be responsible for the actions of their tenants etc. in the same way as other local authorities, such as the heads of clans were. All local structures of lordship should be bound to the crown on equal terms.

Thirdly, they ask that the execution of justice in the matter of compensation for stolen goods, where traditionally the chiefs could have imposed this on those found guilty of offences, should be transferred to the king's forces.

Fourthly, fugitives from the law who have given promise for good behaviour should be pardoned whilst those who refuse to do the same should be publicly named as outlaws.

Fifthly, all landowners and proprietors, 'heritors', were to give bonds to keep the peace before the commissioners.

Sixthly, they asked the Council to act in the case of those landowners who were unable to control the actions their tenants, or members of their families.

Finally, the commissioners sought pardon for thefts and plunder taken before a certain date but, once again, made this dependent upon the clan chiefs bringing in 'dead or alive' some of the most notorious thieves 'of their name'.

It is also worth noting that, in regard to the first proposal above, there was an army which could be used for the purpose proposed. It was the local commissioners that recommended it, but garrisons were expensive and their presence would probably mean occupation rather than consent. It is probable that the reasoning behind the third proposal was to reduce the potential for violence which the local customs entailed. The outcome of the sixth proposal would be that when the traditional ties of lordship or kinship, so strong in the Highlands, were unable to secure peace, new structures emanating directly from the Council were required, because there were no other local institutions strong enough to stand against these ties.

Exercise Now write down what you think these proposals reveal about the government of the region.

Discussion I think there are three main points worth noting.

First, of course, a settled military presence was required, and I expect that you will have listed this. (It suggests that in this region coercion rather than consent was the policy, and whilst this testifies to the increased power of the central government in having such resources at its disposal (it would not have had them at the beginning of the period), it also shows the limited impact that the government had on traditional networks.)

Secondly, I would also expect you to have mentioned the importance of those traditional networks, where kin and clan are regularly referred to in the extract. It is clear from the commissioners' recommendations that these remained very strong in the area.

Thirdly, I would mention the need for equal treatment of all parties, a point which underscores the second, third, and fifth proposals. All should be on the same footing before the law, and not subject to the arbitrary justice of the system of 'hereditary private enterprise' which is suggested by the 'insolences' mentioned in the third proposal.

Clearly the region remained fairly impervious to the interference of central government, whether from London or Edinburgh, and this was a society which could be overcome only by the most brutal of methods in the mid-eighteenth century, when its Jacobite loyalties were used as a reason for destroying its culture.

Distance was also a problem for central government in France, as was language and religion in some areas. Our discussion of the Highlands provides a telling contrast with the way in which the French monarchy absorbed Béarn into the kingdom. Béarn was also an upland region, in the foothills of the Pyrenees, with its own language and distinctive religious tradition, in this case a Protestant Huguenot one. Of course absorption was not achieved without some military action, but there was very little bloodshed and Louis XIII ensured that the Edict of Union of 1620 entailed no immediate revolution in local political and social institutions. Béarn was to retain its customs, rights and privileges; the Estates-General retained its traditional format, and its proceedings continued to be recorded in the local Béarnais language, although French became the language of the law courts. The Estates lost some important powers during the seventeenth century but retained the right to determine noble status within the principality, kept some measure of control over the level of central taxation, and ensured that military service done by the Béarnais was limited to defence of the region. French governmental control was slowly increased by the extension of the venal system of office-holding into the principality, so that gradually the interests of the monarchy and those of the leaders of local society became inseparable. In 1789 the deputies from Béarn could say that, despite becoming part of France only small changes had been made in the life of the province: 'The laws of the region, its liberties, privileges, and rights have been preserved … The general laws of France are entirely foreign to us … We cannot be taxed either collectively or individually without our express consent. We have a national militia with which to protect ourselves' (Desplat, 1991, p.77). This was, of course, a rose-coloured view of the situation, but the fact that local leaders could believe such things illustrates that distance, whether geographical or cultural, need be no barrier when sensitively handled by central government in this period. Absolutist policy was not always neglectful of regional tradition, and the situation in Béarn was not unlike that which we have already noted in Languedoc during the intendancy of Basville, where the interests of the local leadership were skilfully linked to those of the crown.

Towns

In all the countries in Britain and France, towns were distinctive political entities with their own privileges. In earlier parts of the course you will have noted the role played by the urban leadership in the opposition to Charles I on the eve of the civil war, the importance of places like Bordeaux during the Frondes, and the significant part played by towns in the dissemination of literacy and of religious ideas. In addition, not only did they contain such concentrations of population as existed at this time, but they were also the centres of justice and the law courts. Above all towns had developed institutions of self-government covering a wide range of activities. For all these reasons they were a critical element within political society but, as Video 8 points out, there was great variety within the urban landscape. Turn now to Video 8.

Whilst watching the video you will need the *Illustration Book* (Pls 45, 46, 47).

You will remember from TV5 how similar urban functions were expressed in rather different ways at Chipping Campden and Richelieu. (If you cannot remember what was said in TV5, start by reviewing that programme.) In the following exercises we shall look at how in Stirling in Scotland, social divisions are embodied in the development of the town and how in Youghal and Kinsale, in Ireland, urban functions developed during the seventeenth century and may be seen in the buildings.

Video Exercise 1 Watch Part 4 of the video, and using the plan of Stirling (Illustration Book, Pl.45), make notes on:

1   how the topography of the town embodies the social divisions within it;

2   how the functions of the town of Stirling may be seen in the placing and design of the buildings;

3   what changes took place over the seventeenth century in the relative positions of the nobility and the urban élite.

Discussion   1   The levels of the town reflect the status of the residents. At the top of the hill is the royal palace, slightly lower down is Argyll's lodging, lower still is Mar's Work. On the same level is the church and the almshouses.

Below that is the broad street with the market (the mercat cross), the town hall (tollbooth), and merchants' houses, many of which would have had shops on the ground floors.

2   The town is highly zoned. The nobles' houses are nearest the castle; the merchants' houses are in the main business street, with the market cross and the centre of town government (although Bruce's town hall dates from 1703, it replaced an earlier town hall on the same site). The almshouses, donated by a wealthy merchant and commissioned by the town council, lie next to the church, many of whose elders would have been drawn from the merchant élite.

The style of the nobles' houses owes much to influences outside Scotland, to a court culture drawing particularly on French influences, and also displays their status in coats of arms. The houses contain substantial public rooms and ceremonial entrances. The merchants' houses are a marked contrast: domestic in scale, the vaulted ground floors occupied by business premises, sometimes with no access from them to the upper storeys, creating thereby a modest entrance, with vertically ordered living quarters, the style of the buildings drawing on vernacular traditions rather than textbook architecture. However, in their public projects, the merchants were more cosmopolitan in their taste, choosing the king's mason, John Mylne to build the almshouses and William Bruce to build the new tollbooth or town hall, the first classical town hall in Scotland.

3   The buildings of Stirling suggest the growing confidence and predominance of the mercantile élite, scarcely surprising with the departure of the royal court from Scotland. The construction of Mar's work and the earlier parts of Argyll's lodging date from the period when the court occupied Stirling castle. The second phase of building at Argyll's lodging corresponds with Charles I's visit of 1633 to be crowned at Holyrood. The Earl of Stirling, secretary of state for Scotland and owner of the house, was virtual ruler of Scotland in Charles's absence. The third phase of building corresponds with the occupation of the house by the 9th Earl of Argyll, a great noble and commander of a noble fief in the western highlands. During James, Duke of York's residence in Scotland he visited Argyll in Stirling.

Set this beside the development of merchants' houses in the second half of the century and their final expression of confidence in the new tollbooth. It is the merchants who commission the most celebrated architects of the day in Mylne and Bruce. It is they who use the most up-to-date classical style to assert their status in the burgh.

Video Exercise 2   Now watch Part 2 of the video and make notes on how the individual buildings in Youghal and Kinsale reflect changes in the occupation and use of the towns. You will find plans of the towns in the Illustration Book, Pls 46 and 47.

Discussion   Both towns show evidence of older occupancy by the Irish or Old English in Tynte's Castle and the French prison. Both have a concern for defence, though of a rather different type: Youghal has its walls, Kinsale its great fortresses (there was a wall round the landward side of the town in the seventeenth century). Both have charitable magnates giving almshouses: the Earl of Cork at Youghal and Sir Robert Southwell in Kinsale. Both have evidence of the development of English mercantile activity, though in both towns the quays and the waterfront are much altered since the seventeenth century.

In Kinsale there's the centrally placed market hall, with its council chamber above, in Youghal there's the fine merchant's house.

The changes we see are the increasing influence of English settlers and the development of their mercantile activity in the course of the seventeenth century. There is, too, a new perception of the need to defend Ireland as part of the strategic requirements of the British Isles.

We will now return to our more general discussion on towns.

Although the capital cities were occasionally in conflict with central government, especially in mid-century, in general, their interests coincided with those of the state, and it is the provincial towns which are of most interest to us in this unit.

Of 117 municipal corporations in Ireland in 1692 almost two-thirds had been created since the beginning of the century. This fact points out the importance of urban status to the crown, for the creation of towns in Ireland had more to do with politics than economics as the examples of Youghal and Kinsale demonstrate. Towns had the right to send MPs to the Irish parliament, and the creation of boroughs was one means of ensuring that Protestants were elected, especially in Ulster which was the least urbanized part of the country with Londonderry, its largest town, having a population of only 2000. Many of these newly created towns would not be recognized as such by us at all, but the older towns, Cork, Limerick, and Waterford for example, were also important centres of government support, often with garrisons surrounded by a hostile rural environment. (Not unlike the situation in the Highlands.) In Ireland the towns, receiving their privileges as they did from the crown, can be seen as instruments of central government.

There was also considerable growth in the number of Scottish towns in this period, but with an important difference. 'Burghs', as they were called in Scotland, were privileged communities granted rights by the king for internal and external trade, and so were essentially economic entities with their own political structure. These burghs fell into two categories; royal burghs, of which there were about 70 in this period, had control of foreign trade and also had the right to send MPs to parliament, and burghs of barony, often very small communities like Langholm in Dumfriesshire, which were limited to inland trade and, though possessing rights of self-government, had no representation in the wider government of the country. The royal burghs were the most important, and prominent townsmen, merchants and lawyers supported by urban clergy, played significant parts in the opposition to Charles I in 1638 and also to Cromwell in 1650–1. Subsequently, however, the towns tended to identify their economic interests with the increasing prosperity of the nation as indicated at Stirling in the video. Although there was some urban unrest over the Act of Union which left only 15 seats in the British parliament for the Scottish burghs, the leadership of the burghs saw more gain in co-operation than confrontation. They retained their privileges over trade and self-government within their communities and successfully protected their religion, thereby laying the groundwork for what was to become the Scottish Enlightenment later in the eighteenth century.

Figure 22
View of Gloucester, from
Severall Prospects of the
Cheife Citys and Townes in
England and some other
of the cheife citys in
Ewrop by John Overton,
c. *1690. Ashmolean Museum*
Dept of Prints and Drawings.

The Puritan leaders of many of the larger provincial towns in England had played a prominent part in the opposition to crown policy in the decades leading up to the civil war. In cities such as Gloucester and York the corporation had been in conflict with the cathedral chapters, many of whom were Arminian supporters, during the 1630s, and in smaller towns such as Dorchester and Bury St Edmunds the corporation had been outspoken opponents of the Personal Rule. Unlike the JPs, whose commissions were renewed annually, the urban leadership, the aldermen and councillors, often enjoyed office, and the wide range of local authority it brought with it, for life, a privilege which was written in to the town charter. That charter, however, was granted by the crown and Charles I had attempted to interfere in some towns or grant new charters to others, such as Thaxted, in order to build up support for his policy. This had little effect, but it would be wrong to suggest that all towns were opposed to the crown. In some places, such as Oxford and York, there was a powerful faction within the corporation in support of the crown; in others there were divisions between town governors and the people, as at Maidstone, which could be exploited by the crown to its advantage. Nevertheless it is broadly true that, in the earlier part of our period urban magistrates proved to be a considerable source of opposition to royal policy. After 1660 this changed somewhat, partly as a result of the Corporation Act which removed all dissenters from office in towns, and partly because the emergence of party politics at the centre spilled over into the town corporations so that the crown was able to exploit political divisions within towns in order to build up support for its policies. This it did by the granting of fresh charters, not always successfully as James II was to discover, which altered the governing structure of many towns in the 1680s (see Coward pp.377–9). By the end of the period the leadership of most towns were sharing in the general commercial prosperity of the country and, as long as they were able to sustain the privileges of their own community and their own privileges within that community, they were happy to support the crown.

We have already discussed the way in which faction and patronage could affect the government of a large provincial French city in the audio-cassette on Marseille. French towns in this period were of three sorts. They were either under the authority of a local seigneur or lord, or they were corporate towns whose charter vested the government of the town in the leading inhabitants, the bourgeois, or they were communes in which the inhabitants were bound together by an oath recognized by the king or a local lord. Marseille, Toulouse and Bordeaux, which have all been mentioned in this unit, were examples of corporate towns, and as the seventeenth century progressed their institutions became more uniform. After the Ormée the mayoralty of Bordeaux rarely visited the city, and towards the end of the century the number of venal offices was increased so that the crown had ever more close supervision of the Bordelais. In return for this supervision the privileges of the bourgeois were reinforced when access to that status was restricted after 1671. In commune towns, such as Beauvais, the same pattern emerged, with the traditional rights of the commune, which held frequent assemblies, being steadily eroded. This was achieved by the system of venality so that, in 1692, all municipal functions were in the hands of office-holders. At the beginning of the eighteenth century the Captain of

Beauvais, Marshal de Boufflers, became the town governor and executed his office through a hereditary deputy. Although, the inhabitants of Beauvais were able to exploit the venal system by purchasing some offices for themselves, it is true to say that almost all towns in this period came under closer scrutiny by central government, often acting through the agency of a nobleman.

In summary, therefore, we see that tension existed between central and provincial or local government in this period, but it is important to stress that it was not always defined in terms of opposition. The examples of the Scottish Highlands and Béarn show that similar problems did not always lead to similar solutions, whilst a comparison of the treatment of the Highlands with that of Scottish towns also demonstrates that policy was not uniform. Nevertheless, a degree of uniformity was desired by central government and, as the period progressed, that seems to have been echoed by the regional and local leaderships, who were prepared to co-operate with the centre as long as they retained their authority within their own locality and continued to prosper. Careful exercise of patronage could ensure that. In most parts of the British Isles and France the disruptive tensions of the early part of the period had been replaced by a sometimes grudging, but often mutually beneficial compromise between centre and locality. Each needed the other, and even the French office-holders, those quintessential royal servants, had to buy goods from, socialize with, and often marry their children to those neighbours among whom they lived their daily lives

Keeping the peace

So far we have been discussing the relationship between local and regional governors and the centre, but should now look briefly at the local role of the administrators, which can be best defined as keeping the peace and ensuring that taxes were paid.

You may remember that at the end of the last unit on religion we discussed the role of the church courts in the maintenance of morality or, as contemporaries would have described it, 'the reformation of manners'. In England and Wales after the Restoration the church courts lost a good deal of their disciplinary functions, and certainly much of their local status in this respect, and that task had to be taken on by other agencies. Read now *Anthology*, II.23. You will see that the local magistrates, apart from exhibiting the usual xenophobic attitudes to the French, saw themselves in the forefront of moral reform as well as civil peace-keeping. Indeed, it was the former which occupied by far the greater part of the address, but one is almost tempted to say sermon.

Exercise   List the principal offences, in *Anthology*, II.23, identified by the speaker, and their consequences.

Discussion   The sins highlighted as leading to breakdown in local society were swearing, perjury, profaning the Sabbath by working, and drunkenness; and their consequences were listed as debauchery, irreverence to God, and disrespect for government. You may have rearranged sins and consequences in a slightly different order, but the point remains.

It would be difficult to find a more comprehensive statement in support of social control or a clearer indication of the confidence in the magistracy as the proper agency to undertake this task. The tone of the document is as revealing as its content, for it is eloquent testimony to the dominance of the JPs over the government of provincial England. Anthony Fletcher (1986), the most recent historian of Stuart local government, has remarked on their 'unbounded confidence' which was exhibited by 'the manner in which they sought to inculcate a sense of responsibility on the county'. In his final chapter, which he entitles 'The Triumph of the Gentry', he shows how they subsumed and mastered localism for the purposes of government and created a tradition of administrative activism. Thus in England the tension between local and central government had been largely resolved, leaving a legacy of a long and enduringly stable administrative system which still forms the framework of our present, and recently much threatened, structure.

Social control was also an integral part of the Scottish system, but here the county and regional secular authorities were less important than the formally ecclesiastical ones, and in particular the kirk sessions, which also included local laymen. As you can see from Offprint 13 they exercised a close, and to our eyes, intrusive supervision over the lives of the inhabitants, and with a fair degree of success if the rate of convictions is any measure. Local governors in Britain and France operated through different institutions and came from varying social backgrounds, but they shared a concern for the consequences of immorality, which they saw as threatening moral and spiritual stability through deviance, social order through crime, and the economic well being of all through poverty. The way in which those issues were addressed will be discussed in more detail in Unit 9.

References

Bonney, R. (1988), *Society and Government in France under Richelieu and Mazarin, 1624–61*, Macmillan, London.

Desplat, C. (1991), 'Louis XIII and the Union of Béarn to France', in M. Greengrass (ed.) *Conquest and Coalescence; the Shaping of the State in Early Modern Europe*, Edward Arnold, London.

Fletcher, A.J. (1986), *Reform in the Provinces, The Government of Stuart England*, Yale University Press, New Haven.

Macinnes, A.I. (1986), 'Repression and Conciliation: the Highland dimension 1660–1688', *Scottish Historical Review*, 65, pp.167–95.

Mitchison, R (1983), *Lordship to Patronage, Scotland 1603–1745*, Edward Arnold, London.

Mousnier, R. (1984), *The Institutions of France under the Absolute Monarchy, 1598–1789*, vol.2, University of Chicago Press, Chicago.

Unit 9
The local community

Prepared for the course team by Anne Laurence

Contents

Study timetable

Weeks of study	Texts	Video	AC	Set books
2	*Anthology,* II.25–31;	Video 9		Coward, Briggs

Objectives

The objectives of this unit are that:

1   you understand the place of the individual or the household in the local community;

2   you know how state mechanisms might operate in the local community, particularly in relation to the relief of poverty and the prosecution of witchcraft;

3   you understand how communities also regulated themselves;

4   you understand how local communities evolved over the period 1620–1714.

Introduction

This unit is concerned with the ways in which local communities were regulated. In Unit 8 you saw how government operated at provincial level and in Unit 10 you will see how households were regulated. Here, we are concerned with the interaction between the individual (or household) and the wider community, and with the impact of the state on the individual (or household).

In the first part of the unit we shall look at the how local communities were regulated, in the second part of the unit and in the video exercise we shall concentrate upon the relief of the poor as an aspect of controlling the community, and in the third part we shall look at witchcraft.

Regulating the local community

In both Units 1 and 8 you've seen something of the institutions which governed local communities.

Exercise   Thinking about what you have read, what were the principal organizations responsible for administration at the most local level?

Discussion   I would expect you to make the point that in France local communities were governed by assemblies and in England by part-time, semi-amateur officers appointed from the local gentry. In rural Ireland administration depended upon the extent to which Dublin was able to control the area. In rural Scotland the kirk sessions, the parish assembly of minister and lay elders, was responsible for much local administration.

But this was what happened in the countryside (where, as you will remember from AC1, section 1) most of the population of France and the British Isles lived. Larger towns were in all of these places run by corporations, bodies of men (virtually never women) elected on a franchise of urban householders which might be more or less exclusive. Towns were just as much a form of local community as rural societies

In the rest of this section of the unit I want to consider how these mechanisms of local government worked in relation to the local communities they served. We will concentrate on rural communities here and look more at urban communities in the next section.

What was the local community?

In this unit I am going to use the term 'local community' to mean the lowest level of grouping of people beyond the household. In England,

Wales, Lowland Scotland and much of France this often coincided with the parish. In upland regions of France, the Scottish Highlands and much of Ireland it coincided more with clusters of settlement engaged in some common agricultural enterprise, with habitations often widely dispersed and with the community fluctuating greatly in size as inhabitants accompanied their cattle and sheep to upland pastures in the summer.

In TV7 and Video 7 you saw how the church might encompass activities which were not strictly speaking religious, but which were important to the identity of the community. The guild insignia of the sailors and bakers of Burntisland were displayed in the church there, while the prosperous linen merchants of Brittany appropriated the image of a local saint for their guild banner. The livelihoods of the parishioners and the prosperity of the parish were closely identified with the church. Likewise, the administration of the community might be closely linked with the ecclesiastical parish, usually at the behest of the secular government.

Differences between the local communities of France and the British Isles may be emphasized by differences of approach between historians of the different countries. There is really no English equivalent to the study by Gutton (1974). This examines the mechanisms by which French village society operated in the early modern period. Studies of local communities in the seventeenth century are scarce for Scotland, and virtually non-existent for Ireland. Even for England it is difficult to discover how local officials were chosen and much of what is said about Gaelic Ireland and the Scottish Highlands is based upon suppositions about the lack of ecclesiastical organization there, and the resistance of traditional clan-based societies to royal authority.

The administration of the local community

Let us first consider how local communities were administered. We shall look at the various countries in sequence and then at the changes which took place over the period.

Assemblies in different parts of France had different names, often reflecting regional particularism as much as differences of organization. They met five or six times a year, more often if there was some specific piece of business to transact, normally after one of the church services on Sunday, in the village square or market place. Until the Counter-Reformation prohibition on using the church for profane purposes, assemblies often met in the church. The membership was normally all householders, with variations from place to place as to whom was considered to be a householder. Widows were normally the only female householders, but seem rarely to have participated in assemblies. There were strict regulations intended to ensure that the meetings were well attended. However, it was sometimes difficult to get sufficient attenders to conduct the business. At Belleville-sur-Saône eight assemblies were held in 1695: no-one attended all eight, only one person attended seven, and 43 people attended only one of the eight assemblies.

The assembly's only permanent functions were to raise money and men; during peace time it might not be necessary to raise men. Each assembly nominated officers annually. These had various names, most commonly they were called *syndics*, the only one always nominated was someone to collect the *taille*. The number and function of the other officers varied from place to place. Pastoral communities had *syndics* of pastures, vine-growing communities someone to protect vineyards from predators. There were village foresters, cowherds, schoolteachers, wise women and midwives. Someone had to organize labour service to maintain roads. Some communities maintained their own bake houses and mills (like those at the Moulins de Kérouat in Brittany in TV3). The organization of common land was an important function; this might be pasture, forest, marshland or arable land.

The greatest variations between French communities coincided more or less with geographical regions. Northern French communities, where seigneurial control was greatest, differed markedly from the communities of the south, where it was weakest. In southern France assemblies were generally known as *consulats* (or in Bordeaux *jurades*, as we saw in Unit 3) and the elected leaders, often two, as consuls. These communities had a strong tradition of independence and it was here that community institutions were most highly developed. Shepherds, foresters, communal mills, forges and ovens were most likely to be found here. Formal records were kept of meetings and financial accounts were kept and audited annually. In certain regions, notably in mountain regions and on the northern border of France, communal autonomy was particularly strongly defended.

In northern France assemblies were generally known as *échevinages* and their elected leaders as *échevins* or mayors. They were often highly dependent on the local seigneur who might have the right to summon the assembly and to nominate its officers. Assembly and officers counted for little in a community with a powerful seigneur who owned the mill, the forge and the baker's oven. He might control weights and measures and Sunday observance, functions which in the south were more likely to fall to the *consulat*. But a strong seigneur did not necessarily mean a weak assembly; in Burgundy both institutions flourished.

Perhaps the most powerful assemblies were those of the mountain communities where the authority of seigneurs and the crown were weak. There was a high rate of participation and their jurisdiction often covered a very large area, partly because they administered the communal holdings of extensive mountain pastures, essential to the survival of the community. As late as the eighteenth century, up to 80 per cent of land in parts of the Pyrenees was communally owned. Officers took an oath of office and even had a ceremonial hood with a red and black tippet as a badge of office.

In these communities the parish and the assembly often covered the same area, but the priest might have little to do with the assembly except for perhaps helping to appoint a schoolmaster and licensing wise women and midwives. The fabric of the church was usually the responsibility of the community but it was administered by an assembly of vestrymen, who were sometimes members of the assembly. Parishioners did not usually mind maintaining the fabric of the church, but they often objected strongly to finding money for the *presbytère*, where the priest lived.

In Brittany (see TV7 and Video 7), the relationship between the community and the parish was rather different. The vestry and the assembly were often the same body. As the *général de la paroisse* they carried out the functions of both bodies and often exercised considerable control over the church, dictating the times of services and appointing churchwardens. The visible evidence of this is to be seen in the large porches and sacristies of Breton parish churches used for meetings of the assembly. Concerns were voiced that the great burst of church adornment and the building of ossuaries, and calvaries was being funded by money collected from the community which ought properly to be spent on something else.

In the British Isles there was a much greater emphasis on the ecclesiastical parish as a unit of administration. As in France, the parish church was a place for displaying community solidarity and gratitude for good fortune in the form of gifts; it was also a place for displaying symbols of power. Mayoral insignia (as at Youghal in Ireland), special seats for local magistrates (as at Burntisland in Scotland), prominent monuments to local magnates (as at Youghal and Chipping Campden) and the very placing of the church in relation to buildings associated with the economic life of the community and its governors all provide evidence that the parish was a complicated institution in which sacred and secular interacted.

We saw in Unit 1 how in England and Wales local communities were administered by officials. But, as in France, there were assemblies, called vestries, whose functions were concerned with the church. When, in the sixteenth century, the parish became a secular administrative unit, the vestry acquired extra functions. Everyone who paid the church rate (the levy for the maintenance of the fabric of the church) was eligible to be a member and members were nominated from among the most substantial inhabitants. The vestry was required to meet annually to elect two churchwardens. If there was a dispute, the minister might choose one and the parishioners the other. The vestry also chose surveyors of the highway, where they existed. Under the Poor Law of 1601 the vestry was responsible for choosing two overseers of the poor, though many parishes did not appoint such officers until the 1660s. The vestry set the poor rate and the amount of the pensions to be paid to paupers. The parish constable, however, had to be approved by the commission of the peace (the local body of the justices of the peace), but if there was a local manorial court still in existence, that might recommend someone to the justices.

Parish officers were usually drawn from the yeomanry and lesser gentry, people of some financial substance and standing in the community. Churchwardens had to carry out investigations on behalf of the church to check on whether any church laws were being infringed. Not only did they have to provide returns on attendance at church, but they had to indicate whether there were any major infringements by clergy or laity of the church's extensive regulations over personal conduct. They were responsible for identifying adulterers, married people living apart from their spouses, unlicensed surgeons and midwives, as well as failures to fulfil obligations to repair roads, fences or ditches. They provided for the poor who were settled in the parish and receiving pensions, while overseers, where they existed, dealt with casual or occasional paupers. The constable had responsibilities for public order, but he was not a policeman in the modern sense. The prosecution of criminals was the personal responsibility of victims of crime who had to swear a deposition before a magistrate. The constable might report contraventions of local regulations concerning the opening of alehouses, rowdy behaviour and public health, and he and the churchwardens had overlapping authority for highways.

Exercise   What differences can you see between the relationship between parish officers and assemblies in England and France?

Discussion   In France the assembly was more important than its officers, who were simply its agents. It was the assembly which formed the link between the community and higher levels of government – *intendants, parlements* or provincial estates. In England, it was the officers who were the link between the community and higher levels of government, ecclesiastical and secular, not the vestry.

We know very little about how local communities worked in Ireland, especially rural Catholic communities. The areas of the province of Munster settled under the Elizabethan plantation schemes were supposed to have manorial courts and privileges on the English model, though little was done except for the crown's attempts to exact rents and military service from its tenants. Urban boroughs, often very small by English standards, were governed by corporations in which, especially in Munster, Old English Catholics still played an important part. The general policy of the Dublin government was to try to ensure that the administration of the countryside was in the hands of Protestants. High sheriffs, under sheriffs, bailiffs, constables and justices of the peace were recruited from the New English Protestant settlers, but many landowners, including Catholics, complained of the social inferiority of these officers. Indeed, two English justices were prosecuted in 1639 for murdering Englishmen respectively in Bandon and Clonakilty, co. Cork. Shortage of suitable recruits meant that until the 1660s many local officials were in fact Catholics. In parts of the country, especially in the Gaelic lands in the west, English administrators were spread very thinly.

Church of Ireland parishes had little chance of forming the basis of any sort of local community. In the 1620s only one in six even had a preaching minister. The proscription of Roman Catholicism meant that the Catholic churches could not operate openly enough to form the basis of a local community. Priests were maintained by contributions from the devout and a few religious houses of monks and nuns maintained a precarious and more or less clandestine existence.

In 1642 the Scots troops who arrived in Ulster set up a presbytery at Carrickfergus; the ministers were the chaplains to the troops, elders were drawn from the regiments, each of which was a kirk session. Further presbyteries were established in 1644 in Belfast and Route. After the departure of the Scottish troops the presbyteries survived, and some of the social and economic functions of Scottish local government seemed to have appeared in the Ulster Presbyterian system.

It is in the organization of Scottish communities that we see the greatest coincidence between church and community. The kirk session was the assembly of the minister and lay elders for each parish. Its functions were similar to those of the English churchwardens: enquiring into the moral state of the parishioners, and supervising attendance at church and the provision of education. Although justices of the peace on the English model were introduced in Scotland in 1609 their powers were more restricted. Local nobles retained considerable powers over their tenants. In the famine of 1623 the Scottish Privy Council found it difficult to implement satisfactory measures for relief because of the absence of a country-wide system of local administration. It was not until the middle of the seventeenth century that the kirk became effective in the most distant parts of the country. A visitation of the parish of Lochalsh in the Highlands in 1649 found that the church had nothing but bare walls. The parishioners were charged with roofing and flooring the church, glazing the windows, and providing a pulpit, stool of repentance and reading desk.

Changes in the administration of the community, 1620–1714

There were considerable changes in the operation of local government in the period 1620–1714, many of them in response to changes in central government. In France and England and Wales there seems to have been a tendency towards more oligarchic control. Local assembly and vestry members and local officers were drawn from an increasingly restricted range of people. In France this coincided with the extension of the power of *intendants* and the erosion of the powers of provincial bodies – *parlements* and provincial estates – to whom village assemblies had been answerable. It also coincided with more communities appointing permanent officers. The interests of the crown and the community coalesced in diminishing the role of the seigneur in those regions where they had been powerful.

The changes in France were in part the result of attempts made to end communal indebtedness. We have seen how burdensome were taxes on local communities in the 1630s and 1640s and many communities had to borrow money to pay taxes. Any slight reverse, such as a poor harvest or a flood, pushed them into insupportable debt. Even under Mazarin, some communities had to be allowed to write off their debts. In 1665 a royal edict required all communities to have their debts assessed by the *intendant* who would agree a repayment plan with the local assembly. Small debts were to be met by a *taille* levy, larger debts were to be met by such measures as the sale of communal property. Restrictions were placed on further borrowing. The sale of communal property resulted in a marked change in the structure of local communities. Land was sold to non-resident landlords and to the wealthiest people in the village, accentuating social divisions in the community. The state, in the form of the *intendants*, thus acquired a stronger foothold in the local community and this tended to increase the separation between its religious and secular functions.

In England and Wales the tendency towards more oligarchic control of local communities coincided with the decline in the church courts and with economic changes which accentuated differences in wealth between country-dwellers. Increasing numbers of people became dependent upon wages for their livelihoods. These landless labourers were employed by landowners – yeomen or gentry – whose land holdings were increasing in size and being farmed more intensively with cash crops.

The most catastrophic changes took place in Ireland and Scotland as a result of the political and religious upheavals there. In Ireland, the settlement following the Williamite wars and the Treaty of Limerick of 1691 resulted in the proportion of profitable land owned by Catholics declining from 22 per cent in 1688 to 14 per cent in 1703. The composition of the landowning class did not substantially change: to a large extent those Protestant landowners who already owned land simply enlarged their properties. But the other result of the settlement was the extension of common law courts and justices of the peace to the whole country and the imposition of penal laws which prevented Catholics from holding any office. Although much local administration remained pretty rudimentary, it was only after 1691 that it explicitly excluded all Catholics regardless of their social status or property. Yet taxation was levied on the occupation not the ownership of property, so Catholic tenants who occupied the land owned by Protestants had to pay taxes to support a government from which they were totally excluded.

In Scotland, too, it was the upheavals following William's assumption of the English crown which upset local government. This was for two reasons: the conflict within the Church of Scotland and the continuation of opposition to William in the Highlands. As you will remember, the Church of Scotland was organized as a Presbyterian church, with a hierarchy of assemblies from the kirk sessions up to the governing body, the General Assembly of the kirk, but it also had bishops. In 1688 many Scottish bishops found themselves unable to accept the deposition of James VII and II and in 1690 a strong anti-episcopalian party in the church achieved a new religious settlement without bishops. Over 600 ministers were excluded from the church and without a minister no elders could be ordained so kirk sessions could not continue. These problems were compounded by the Jacobite war and by famine in the mid-1690s. Although the church did settle down and parishes acquired new ministers, local communities were seriously disrupted by ecclesiastical divisions, war and famine and it was some time before the administration of local communities returned to any sort of order.

The poor and the problem of poverty

In this section of the unit we shall look at how the problem of poverty was perceived and at attempts to deal with it. We shall see how the interests of the state, the community and the individual intersected. So far, we have concentrated upon rural communities, but much of the surviving evidence relates to poverty in the towns, so we shall concentrate here on towns.

The problem of poverty

Why should early modern states concern themselves with the poor when they did not regard social policy in the modern sense as being their responsibility? The short reply is that the poor had a considerable capacity for causing civil disorder. Tax riots, as we have seen, caused disruption in France. There were also riots in many places in France and the British Isles which occurred when bread or grain became too expensive for ordinary people to afford. In 1630 mobs looted shops during bread riots in Poitiers and in 1693 women in Oxford market pelted millers, mealmen and bakers with stones because of the high price of flour. In 1699 the

Figure 23
The Orphans Crye, *woodcut preface to Michael Sparke,* The Poore Orphans Court or Orphans Cry, *London, 1636, showing orphans crying out for help while others lie dying in the street.* British Library c.95.aa.3, *reproduced by permission of the British Library Board.*

magistrates of Lyon were jostled by a mob complaining at the price of grain. But these were trivial matters of public order by comparison with longer-term recessions which put large numbers of people out of work, and sent whole families onto the roads in search of food and work, often moving from the countryside into the towns.

By the late sixteenth century the provision for unfortunates was in a considerable state of disarray in both Protestant and Catholic countries, a disarray increased by the rising demand for relief during the hard times of the 1590s. For the early seventeenth-century state, then, the problem of the poor was one of preventing the disorder that arose from having masterless men and their families wandering, uncontrolled, around the countryside looking for food and work. Governments, therefore, sought to regulate the freedom of vagrants to wander at will.

Exercise   Turn now to *Anthology*, II.25. What evidence can you find here of:

1   the type of people who were vagrants;

2   the attitude of the authorities to vagrancy.

Discussion   1   These people were clearly very poor, living on the absolute edge of subsistence. The only occupations which are mentioned – chapwoman and tinker – were those where people could only just scrape a living. The chapwoman (a chapman or woman is a peddler, an itinerant seller of small goods) and her daughter were accused of using counterfeit coin, two others were begging. Some of these people were wandering on their own, some in groups. The tinker and his family were driven to vagrancy by straitened circumstances; the runaway apprentice took to the road from misery.

2   There is a strong moral element in the attitude of the authorities. They were very alert to the possibility of sexual licence (as in the case of Margaret Cheeke and Martin Drake); of criminal activity (as in the case of Elizabeth Griffen and her daughter); of breaking rules such as apprenticeship indentures (as in the case of Richard Flower). Simply being a vagrant could provoke punishment (as in the case of Thomas Coxe and his family), but did not automatically do so (as in the case of Nathaniel Leache). You can see that underpinning the rules about of vagrancy was the idea that everyone had a place of origin and that it was the responsibility of that place to look after its own people.

It is difficult to believe that the majority of poor people were wandering about the country or gathering in towns in search of food and work. Much more widespread was the poverty of ordinary people who simply could not support themselves and their dependants. These people were living in communities, without enough to eat and without enough money to pay such demands as might be made of them. A disproportionate number of them were women: young women who could not work because they had a young child (though the illegitimacy rate was low); women widowed with young families; older women with illnesses or disabilities. Old age was not itself considered to constitute a reason for stopping work and there were no pensions for people simply on reaching a certain age; what tended to happen was that older people took on different types of work – women span and men worked as watchmen or doormen. Orphaned children and men disabled by service in the army or at sea or in accidents at work all needed some sort of support. Some of these people needed permanent pensions, others needed support for a period of their lives when they were in particular difficulties. Unlike vagrants, such people were generally considered to be deserving of support and to be eligible for charitable relief. But how such support was administered varied greatly from place to place and the philosophy underlying such relief tells us a good deal about the nature of relations between the state and its subjects.

Attitudes to the poor in all the countries we are considering were influenced by the desire to distinguish between deserving and undeserving. This is clearly shown in the sixteenth-century legislation which formed the basis for poor relief in England in the seventeenth century, and in the way it was implemented locally. It is also evident in the development of the *hôpital général* in France from the middle of the century. Relieving poor people rather than removing the conditions which gave rise to poverty was the principal object of both state legislation and private charity. Distinctions of status were recognized, the poor were not afforded opportunities to better themselves and those people of higher social status who had fallen on hard times were recognized in France in the category of *pauvres honteux* (shamefaced poor) and given money discreetly.

Records of the poor

Ostensibly we are dealing with a group of people of whom one would expect to find little record, but the state's concern with the poor and the development of mechanisms and institutions to deal with them has meant that we sometimes know more about them than we know about slightly better-off people.

The existence of a body of national legislation concerning the poor in England meant that there was a good deal of record-keeping. In Unit 1 we saw how the poor rate, the tax levied on householders to support the poor, was collected. Many places, especially towns, have records relating to the assessment and collection of the tax, though in smaller rural parishes no poor rate was collected until after 1660. There were also censuses of the poor by municipal authorities, and records of disbursements which go into considerable detail as to the kinds of people who claimed poor relief. English records emphasize poor relief collected in the form of a tax and disbursed in the parish in the form of payments or assistance to people at home. Many of these records were for towns because the problem of poverty was generally more acute there, but is easy to see how the system was applied in rural parishes and there exist plenty of records of payment by rural overseers of the poor and churchwardens.

In Scotland very similar legislation to deal with the poor was introduced in the late sixteenth century as Scotland similarly suffered under the recession of the 1590s. But much of the legislation passed was more advisory than mandatory and its administration was given to kirk sessions. Scottish records emphasize the role of the kirk in dealing with the poor, but provision was substantially confined to those parishes with an effective kirk session, something which many parishes did not acquire until later in the seventeenth century. The presbytery of Dingwall, made up of parishes covering much of the northern and western Highlands, ordered a visitation of the parishes of Kintail, Lochalsh and Lochcarron in 1649. After enquiring about the religious provision for the parishes, the visitors asked whether there were collectors and collections for the poor and a poor box. They found that generally these parishes were without any provision for poor relief. The responsibilities of the kirk sessions were both secular and religious for there was a particular duty to help the poor to further the creation of a godly commonwealth on earth. Scottish justices of the peace were responsible for dealing with vagrants but, as we have seen, their role as law enforcers was not well developed.

In both England and Scotland there were private charities, either medieval foundations usually taken over by civic authorities, or new foundations often funded from mercantile wealth. Some charities were simply in the form of disbursements or handouts of food or clothing. Substantial gifts left their mark in almshouses like those in Chipping Campden, Corsham and Stirling.

In Ireland such private charity was virtually the only provision for the poor, and was largely confined to towns and to Protestants. Almshouses such as those in Youghal and Kinsale and charities such as those recorded on the walls of Youghal church provided for local Protestants. Doles (money payments) could be restricted to Protestants by the device of requiring that they be collected at the church door; Catholics were excommunicated from their own church for entering a Protestant churchyard. Attempts to introduce elements of the English poor law were largely unsuccessful except in response to particular crises, as in Dublin in the 1620s when a Book of Orders was issued to JPs, and the export of grain was prohibited. So the record of poor relief in Ireland emphasizes its urban and Protestant character.

In France, especially after 1656, there developed large, centralized urban institutions, with officials, trustees and registers of admissions. There is a wealth of information about the poor interned in them, but very little about the poor who remained at home. Since legislation required that all towns provide *hôpitaux généraux* and, as we heard in AC1, section 1, more of the population of France lived in towns in France than in England, such institutions reached a relatively high proportion of the poor.

These differences in surviving evidence have perhaps exaggerated the differences in the kinds of relief available to the poor between France and England. Let us now look at what was provided for the poor.

The relief of poverty

I've suggested that England had a national system of poor relief through the late sixteenth-century legislation known as the Poor Law. But that is a far cry from everyone actually having access to poor relief. It was not until the 1620s that many places had any formally organized out-relief given to people at home. And it was not until the 1660s that the poor rate, the tax which paid for this relief, was levied on as many as a half of all house-holders. Slack (1988, p.207) has argued that statutory provision had only a marginal impact until the middle of the century. In poor parishes statutory relief might amount to very little, so private charity remained important.

Private charity might be of two types: generalized gifts to the poor to be given out in the form of money, bread, fuel or clothing to deserving members of the parish; or the endowment of an almshouse to provide accommodation and often a small income for a number of poor people or a school for orphan or pauper children. Sums left for such purposes might be very small, a gift of sixpence once a year to four poor people, or large, an almshouse for twenty people.

Kent, a county well endowed with charities in the middle ages, had, by the end of the seventeenth century, almshouse provision for 687 people, some 300 places having been endowed during the sixteenth and seventeenth centuries. Seventeenth-century foundations included that of the yeoman Arthur Willard, who endowed an almshouse for two poor widows at Westerham and that of Abraham Colfe, who left money in 1658 for almshouses at Lewisham to be administered by the London Company of Leathersellers. Each of the five residents was to have a principal room of 12 feet by 15 feet with a fireplace, a small buttery and a 16 foot garden plot. In addition to this almshouse provision, there was charitable support for over a thousand families in Kent.

Contrast this with Lancashire, a large and relatively populous county, but with its population very unevenly distributed. The county had less private charitable provision for the poor in the later middle ages than any English county except the two smallest counties (Huntingdonshire and Rutland) and Westmorland (which consisted largely of Pennine uplands). The charitable impulse in Lancashire seems at first sight to have been unusually weak, only a third of that for a county with a similar population, Hampshire. But a closer look at the benefactions reveals that much may be explained by the geography of the county. The uneven distribution of population and the lack of parochial organization in the Pennine uplands led to the concentration of charitable activity in the more populous and better organized parishes. In 1650 Lancashire had 62 parish churches and 128 chapels. These chapels, many of which were hardly used and had no minister, had been founded in the sixteenth and early seventeenth centuries to provide the most distant parts of the county with a Protestant ministry, even so Lancashire was slow to accept parochial organization and it was the county with the largest numbers of Catholic recusants. Probably 190 communities had some sort of institutional parish life, but charities were distributed very unevenly. Ninety-eight per cent of all endowments went to just over half (103) of the communities; and 36 remote and underpopulated parishes had no charitable provision at all. By the end of the seventeenth century accommodation in almshouses had been endowed for 12 men, 6 women and 14 poor people whose sex was not specified.

The study of provision for the poor in Lancashire by Jordan (1962), the historian of English charities, may be suggestive for other parts of the

British Isles and for France. Lancashire was very unevenly populated. In the Pennine uplands the population was widely dispersed, sometimes formed into hamlets, sometimes distant hill farmers, certainly living in circumstances where people were in no position to collect a weekly bread dole, for example. This situation of uneven provision with little for the poorest and most distant rural areas and reasonable provision for towns must have been replicated in Scotland, Ireland and Wales. In Scotland some attempt was made to introduce statutory poor relief in the more distant parts of the country, as we have seen, but it was not until the eighteenth century that there was any serious attempt to introduce a national system of poor relief in Ireland.

Private charity was given by richer people throughout Christendom as their Christian duty. Sir John Foulis, a gentleman involved in public affairs in Scotland in the later seventeenth century, meticulously recorded his outgoings. He paid his 'teind' or tithe to the minister, £8; he paid £1 8s 'to the beggars when my son Adam was baptized' and a further £1 8s to the poor at the church door; he gave £2 16s to his wife 'to give the poor box, this first Sunday she went to church after her delivery'. He also gave sums to beggars, to his wife to distribute to the poor on unspecified occasions, and further sums on days of thanksgiving or fasting. You may find similar kinds of charitable giving amongst many public-spirited individuals in many countries.

As we have seen, almshouses provision was unevenly distributed over the British Isles, but was important within the individual communities fortunate enough to possess it. Turn now to Video 9. (You will need your *Anthology* and Illustration Book when working on this video.)

Video Exercise 1 Watch Part 1 of the video and make a note of the common features of the buildings you see. You will find it useful to look at the Illustration Book, Pls 45 and 47, and 48, 51 and 53.

Discussion 1 None of the almshouses accommodates more than twelve people, they're all intended to serve relatively small communities.

2 All the buildings are modest, domestic in scale and rather old-fashioned, drawing on the tradition of vernacular building rather than élite building.

3 There is a strong emphasis on religion, in the positioning of the building relative to the church or in the provision of religious services or in religious texts.

4 The patrons are usually lavishly commemorated either in a portrait or, more commonly, in inscriptions and coats of arms.

Video Exercise 2 Now read *Anthology*, II.26 and when you have done that, watch Part 2 of the video, making notes on:

1 The ways in which the buildings embody Lady Hungerford's regulations. You may wish to consult the plan in the Illustration Book (Pl. 53).

2 The kinds of life the inmates are expected to lead.

Discussion 1 Lady Hungerford's regulations are clearly carried out in the buildings. The buildings themselves (almshouse, master's house and schoolhouse), the outbuildings, woodyards and gardens are all laid out as the regulations provide. The poor people are well provided for with money, clothing and accommodation.

2   The inmates are expected to be people of 'an honest life and conversation', industrious and preferably single. But matters are not left at this. There's a high degree of control and direction to ensure that the almspeople remain honest and godly, for example provisions to stop them stealing wood, to attend church, prayers and the bi-annual reading of the rules in the schoolhouse; to prevent drunkenness, swearing, fornication, heresy, and gambling or dissension between the inhabitants; to rise early and work. There's a good deal of supervision: by the vicar (in the requirement to attend church); by the schoolmaster (in the requirement to attend prayers in the schoolhouse) and by Lady Hungerford herself (in the requirement to hear a repetition of the sermon at 'the great mansion house in Corsham').

Notice how godliness, morality and control are almost inseparable and are to be promoted by a combination of decent housing, supervision and punishment.

Video Exercise 3   Now read *Anthology*, II.27(A) and watch Part 3 of the video, making notes on:

1   How provision for the poor is organized at La Salpêtrière.

2   The similarities to, and differences from, Corsham. (You may find the plan in the Illustration Book, Pl. 55 useful.)

Discussion   1   This measure, to judge both from the tone of the edict and from the buildings themselves, is seen more in terms of policing than philanthropy. Religion is important, look at the scale of the chapel and its prominent position in the scheme. The edict mentions the fact that many of the poor have not been baptized and are ignorant of religion. The buildings are not simply intended to provide shelter for people living in Parisian society but are intended to separate them from it as a source of vice. To keep them away from vice they are to work. Notice how God is invoked as punishing everyone for the beggars' crimes.

2   As similarities I would suggest that in both foundations there is a concern with control and with keeping the poor out of trouble. A similar prominence is given to the benefactors of the buildings (Cardinal Mazarin and Lady Hungerford) and the importance of religion is clear in the chapel and schoolroom.

As differences I would suggest that whilst the emphasis at Corsham is on moral regulation, at La Salpêtrière it is more concerned with policing and public order – there is a prison included in the complex. At Corsham inmates were expected to remain there until they died, unless expelled for bad behaviour. At La Salpêtrière many of the inmates were there for only a few weeks.

You might argue that these differences may be accounted for by the different situations of the two institutions. Corsham was a small market town, with a powerful local magnate providing for six members of the local population. Paris was the largest city in Europe with a substantial population of poor people of its own as well as being a magnet for the poor from other parts of the country. However, it is significant that London had nothing analogous to the *Hôpital Général*.

Five hospitals for the sick were founded in London in the sixteenth century and accommodated some 1,000 people. One of them, Bridewell, had additional functions as a workhouse and house of correction and was to form a model which all English counties were instructed to adopt in 1610. These Bridewells were houses of correction for 'the keeping, correcting and setting to work of ... rogues, vagabonds, sturdy beggars and other idle and disorderly persons' (Slack, 1988, p.128). By 1630 most counties and some towns had such institutions. Prison was a place only for holding people pending trial, so magistrates might sentence people to periods in a house of correction, often of only a few days at a time, where they were set to work. Some towns, like Salisbury, attempted to establish workhouses. In the early seventeenth century the impetus to do so was largely from Puritans and few schemes were successful; in the later seventeenth century rather more such projects were introduced as corporations of the poor, often workhouses for children, partly inspired by the example of France.

Dublin was more forward than most places in Ireland in making some kind of provision for its poor, but much of this was in response to the rapid growth of its population in the later seventeenth century. The public affront of the large number of beggars prompted schemes to build a hospital (1669) and a hospital and free school (1671). Both were to be composite institutions providing for adults and children. In fact it proved difficult to mix the functions and the earlier foundation became a workhouse (later a foundling hospital) and the later one a school. In 1713 a hospital for the sick was founded by Dr Steevens and his sister, though it was not ready to admit patients until the 1730s.

The incarceration of the poor in France

In the French countryside there were many forms of relief for the unfortunate. Alms were distributed at funerals and christenings; hostels gave food and shelter to passing travellers. Round Lyon, for example, most parishes had some kind of provision mainly dating from the middle ages. During the early seventeenth century there were attempts to rationalize charitable provision and to institute mechanisms for distinguishing between deserving and undeserving poor. (Medieval institutions generally provided charity indiscriminately.) The collection of taxes for the support of the poor, the registration of people in receipt of relief and the administration of out-relief were all reorganized. But from the 1620s much of the poor relief provision was absorbed into residential institutions. The associations of devout laymen and women, founded under the inspiration of St Francis de Sales and St Vincent de Paul, laid a great stress on visiting the sick, but it is not clear how much material assistance they gave.

Most French towns had a variety of residential institutions whose functions were not clearly differentiated. They served the sick, those unable to support themselves because of illness or infirmity, and orphaned children. They also administered some out-relief. During the seventeenth century there was an attempt to rationalize these institutions, most of which had passed from the control of the religious orders to lay control in which the municipal authorities played an important part.

In 1614 in Lyon a single institution, the *hôpital général,* was created which was at once workhouse, infirmary, orphanage and prison. Those unable to look after themselves were cared for, the able-bodied were set to work, either at the various tasks needed to feed and clothe the inmates or at winding silk. Orphaned children served their apprenticeships there. A world apart was created where the poor were segregated from the life of the city. New admissions were referred by organizations dispensing out-relief in a concerted attempt to prevent begging. There was a chapel and a chaplain who instructed the children, conducted services and catechized the adults. The *hôpital général* in Lyon provided the model for La Salpêtrière in 1656.

Figure 24
La Charité in Lyon, mid-seventeenth century, woodcut in Institution de l'Aumone Générale de Lyon, *1647, 5th. edn. Bibliothèhque Nationale de France.*

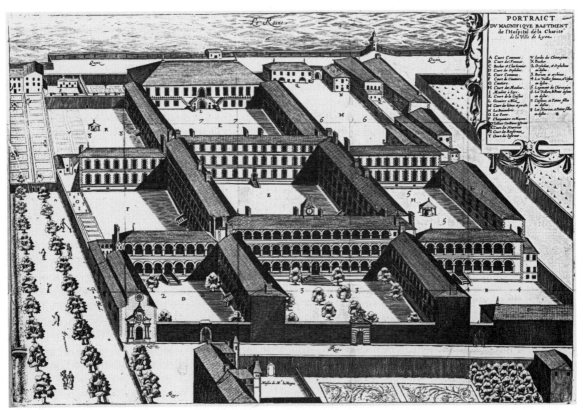

Exercise   Now turn to *Anthology,* II.27(B). What are the implications of this edict?

Discussion   The model of the *hôpital général* at Lyon and at La Salpêtrière was regarded as one which every French town should emulate. No funds were allocated to this work.

Two reasons are offered for this being a desirable move. The first is that La Salpêtrière was overburdened with inmates from the provinces. (If you remember the video, by the 1660s some 4,000 people were accommodated there.) Also, the provision for out-relief in Paris was stretched beyond all reasonable limits. The second is that beggars were 'the most forsaken of human beings' and the function of the *hôpital général* was not simply to set them to work, but also to instruct them in the Christian religion.

The philosophy of this edict, that known as *'l'enfermement des mendiants'* ('the incarceration of beggars'), was adopted throughout France. Medieval institutions were amalgamated, closed down or adapted to provide each city with an institution in which all the poor might be enclosed, away from the population at large. Aix-en-Provence, which in 1600 had places for about 250 people in infirmaries, by the later seventeenth century (when its population was about 29,000) could accommodate 700 to 800 beggars in its *hôpital général*.

By the late seventeenth century many French towns had such institutions, all formed from local initiatives and run entirely by local people from local funds. Increasingly, in a reversal of the developments of the sixteenth century, the day-to-day administration of *hôpitaux* was taken over by religious orders. In 1670 an *hôpital général* was founded in the small cathedral town of Tulle:

> ... to lodge, shut up and feed poor, sick beggars native to these parts or resident here for a year, as also children orphaned or born to beggars, to be instructed in piety and Christian religion and to be made competent in a trade to prevent them from becoming vagrants. (Petit and Mathieu, 1911, p.ii)

However, the poor of Tulle were not completely separated from the life of the town. The *hôpital général* had a monopoly of providing furnishings for funerals and its inmates paraded in public at burials, carrying torches. In 1679 the *hôpital* contained 11 male and 12 female invalids and 19 male and 15 female healthy poor people together with an almoner, menservants and sisters to look after the inmates, with the services of a physician, a priest and a business manager. After the revocation of the Edict of Nantes in 1685 *hôpitaux généraux* were charged with taking in Protestants and converting them, so the *hôpital*, apart from sick people, abandoned children and petty criminals, also contained Huguenots. Increasingly, *hôpitaux généraux* took in a wide variety of people, often for quite short periods.

The move in France to incarcerate the poor, especially from 1662, had some impact on the British Isles. The revolutionary governments of England mooted a number of schemes in the 1650s to increase control over the poor and in the late seventeenth and early eighteenth centuries there was a move to establish workhouses in a number of cities (e.g. Salisbury, Norwich, Exeter and Dublin). The impact of these developments was limited, partly because England was still a much less urbanized country than France and the provisions of the Elizabethan Poor Law for out-relief remained the basis for most of the provision of poor relief. Only in one particular respect was it substantially amended. In 1662 the Act of Settlement clarified the definition of place of origin by parish, but it also recognized that having served an apprenticeship in a parish or occupying property worth £10 a year or more might confer rights of residency. This provision recognized the need to distinguish between controlling vagrants and allowing the active workforce reasonable mobility.

The poor and the authorities

Historians have for long debated the philosophy behind *'l'enfermement des mediants'*. Was it, as Michel Foucault (1961) has suggested, an attempt to isolate the poor, to prevent the moral contagion of their idleness and immorality from affecting the population at large? Was it punitive? Was it an attempt to reform people's natures?

There are two clear explanations and many more unclear ones. Renaissance humanist concepts of civic duty and responsibility as set out by Juan Luis Vives influenced the approach of poverty of both Protestant and Catholic authorities. At the same time, the emphasis on individual acts of almsgiving of the medieval Catholic church declined. Gifts to institutions and town taxes replaced individual gifts and charitable acts. Salvation by works could as well be achieved by a gift to the Sisters of Charity as by seeking out a needy individual. For Puritans and in Protestant parts of France before 1685, relieving poverty was associated with creating a godly commonwealth. Poor co-religionists must be helped as a religious duty, but the benefit was to the soul of the recipient rather than the donor. This philosophy did not create the English Poor Law system but the connection between the administration of poor relief and the parish was not simply an accident of local administration.

Ostensibly we have, by the later seventeenth century, two systems for relieving the poor in England and France with very different emphases on the place of the poor in the community. In England the poor remained part of the community, though they might, if recalcitrant, be punished by a period in a house of correction. In France, there was an increasing move to concentrate the poor in towns and to segregate them in *hôpitaux généraux*. We appear here to have one highly devolved system, the English system based on parishes, and one highly centralized system reflecting the concentration of royal authority in the king. But in their actual administration the very reverse is the case. No French *hôpital général* was founded, governed or funded by anyone but the local town government. Even the instruction of 1662 was not absolute and there were many differences in the institutions to be found in individual towns. In both Aix-en-Provence and Grenoble, for example, many private charities survived. Contrast this with England where, although the administration of the Poor Law was by locally appointed officials (churchwardens and overseers of the poor), they were drawn from a narrow range of the population and they were subject to exact instructions from the statutes and from the Books of Orders issued to justices of the peace. The awesome authority implied by the Salpêtrière buildings contrasted with the cosiness of the almshouses in English villages lulls us into a false sense of how the poor were controlled.

Witches and witchcraft

Informal controls

So far, we have looked at formal mechanisms for governing local communities, but controlling a community isn't just about formal organizations. It is also about social relations, informal hierarchies and relationships, the resolution of disputes and the censure of people who offended against local custom. Let us look at an example, from Shropshire.

Exercise   Richard Gough, a Shropshire yeoman, reported that:

> There happened a difference between John Downton of Alderton, and William Formeston about the right of kneeling in the sixth pew on the south side of the north aisle, and John Downton put a lock on the pew door. But William Formeston ... who claimed a share in the seat, came on the Lord's day following, and giving the pew door a sudden pluck, broke off the lock. Upon this there was a parish meeting appointed (for then there were no ecclesiastical courts held in England) [this was 1658] to decide the controversy, and to settle persons in vacant seats; for it was held a thing unseemly and undecent that a company of young boys, and of persons that paid no leawans [church rates], should sit above those of the rest of the parish. (Gough, 1981, p.117)

What does this account tell us about relations in the community?

Discussion   It tells us that the connections between the ecclesiastical and the secular are impossible to disentangle. It tells us that status and honour were highly valued. It tells us that the community regarded the resolution of this dispute as its responsibility.

This is a dispute about where people sat in church and the last sentence tells us that there was a strong sense of hierarchy embodied in the seating arrangements. Those who paid church rates had better seats than those who did not. We do not know if the assembly called was the vestry or the whole village, but this is a very rare reference to the operation of a parish meeting in England.

There were other ways in which people who offended against the community might be censured. Charivaris or rough music were demonstrations against individuals who were believed to be immoral. Similar acts are found in both France and England. Neighbours gathered, usually at night, the men often dressed as women, and, banging pots and pans, they would shout outside the victim's house. Cuckolds were mocked by horns being hung on their houses or by a demonstrator wearing a pair of horns and accompanied by people chanting satirical rhymes.

There were also days of communal misrule, when conventional hierarchies were overturned. Commonly this was a procession of young men, led by a lord of misrule, parading through the village calling shame on offenders. The authorities increasingly saw such customs as pagan peasant survivals. In France some authorities tried to abolish them, in other places priests tried to harness them by using lords of misrule to raise money for the church. In England, Puritan disapproval led to the decline of such processions in the 1650s. After the Restoration in 1660 they were increasingly replaced by anti-Catholic demonstrations – bonfires and the burning of effigies of the pope on 5 November (the anniversary of the Gunpowder Plot) and 17 November (the anniversary of Queen Elizabeth's accession).

Exercise   Read Briggs, pp.189–96. What changes does Briggs suggest took place in French popular culture during the seventeenth century?

Discussion   Briggs identifies two main developments. He suggests that there was an increasing contempt for popular culture amongst the ruling élite and thus a polarization into two cultures, one popular and regional and the other élite and national.

At the same time, he also suggests that in some areas of life a greater uniformity was achieved by the work of the authorities. He cites the church's attempts to regularize marriage and the limited success in controlling communal disorder. The most complete change was in the way in which the official persecution and burning of witches came to an end.

Witchcraft: the mental world of the seventeenth century

In this section of the unit we shall look at what is to many modern observers one of the most inexplicable characteristics of early modern society. We shall concentrate upon witchcraft not as the subject of a learned literature but rather as an aspect of relations within local communities.

Exercise   From what you have just read in Briggs (pp.192–6) note down the ways in which local communities regarded witchcraft.

Discussion   Briggs points to the fact that witchcraft was essentially a local phenomenon and something in which nearly everyone believed as a matter of course. Only in extreme cases, were witches taken to court, a more effective remedy was often believed to be counter-magic. Most witches had a long-standing reputation as such and only where exceptional malevolence was suspected were official processes invoked against them.

Exercise   Now read Coward, pp.75–7. What differences do you notice between French and English witchcraft?

Discussion   Coward suggests that a significant difference was the absence of charges relating to pacts with the devil or the wearing of distinctive clothing amongst those accused of witchcraft in England. Briggs mentions the importance of diabolic pacts in French accusations and also suggests that a wider range of hostile acts lay behind French accusations than English accusations.

What is very striking is how similar are the descriptions of witchcraft in both countries. Small communities beset by internal disputes used a belief in supernatural powers to identify people responsible for causing harm. English historians are inclined to believe that England was the great exception in Europe for the mildness of its witch panics. But recent work on different regions of France suggests increasingly that the incidence of witch hunting there may well have been exaggerated.

Since most of evidence of witchcraft comes to us through witch trials, let us look at how the law regulated these matters in England and Wales.

Exercise   Read now *Anthology*, II.28. What do we learn from this about the English government's attitude to witchcraft?

Discussion   At first sight we notice the repeal of earlier legislation. Is this the dawn of a new age of relaxation? Not a bit of it. It is the necessary prelude for 'the better restraining' and 'more severe punishing' of those found guilty of committing the offences of 'conjuration', 'witchcraft' and 'dealing with evil and wicked spirits'. But this measure was not just an attempt to limit the incidence; witchcraft was to be 'utterly avoided, abolished and taken away'.

Let us now look at what kinds of offence the act is actually talking about. What were people complaining of when they went to the authorities and said that someone was a witch (which is how most prosecutions came about)? The act gives us some clue. Invoking or communicating with evil spirits, feeding or employing such spirits are specified first. So someone laying a place at table for someone who was not present, or talking to someone not there might find themselves charged. Using supernatural means to kill or harm another person or helping such a person were offences. But these were not offences which might just result in a fine or imprisonment (neither of them penalties much used in early modern England and Wales). They carried a mandatory death penalty and (I would not expect you to know this) it was not possible to invoke the only form of mitigation open to those charged with a felony, benefit of clergy. There was a secondary category of offences which did not carry the death penalty, but which carried a punishment much more characteristic of the English seventeenth-century judicial system, one involving public shame: the pillory and public confession. Divining or charming carried such penalties for the first offence.

As you can see, this is an English act; it was the measure which governed the prosecutions of alleged witches in England and Wales until it was repealed in 1736. Its passing had a good deal to do with the accession of

James I to the throne of England because of his interest in witchcraft. Certain of the act's features were common to such measures in other countries. Most countries relied on the evidence of confessions, but the means by which these were exacted differed according to the system of law. The civil or Roman law practised in France and Scotland was inquisitorial. Suspects were questioned by the magistrates or judges and confessions were the culmination of this process. The common law of England, Wales and Ireland was adversarial and the assumption of innocence restricted the judiciary's power to exact a confession. The prosecution of someone as a witch did not remove them from the community into an impersonal criminal justice system, they remained in many important respects the responsibility of the community. *Anthology*, II.29 shows that this responsibility had financial implications. The cost of persecuting and executing a witch in Scotland was considerable.

Figure 25
Illustration to a tract written by Matthew Hopkins, the 'Witch-Finder General', The Discovery of Witches: In Answer to severall Queries, Lately delivered to the Judges of Assize for the county of Norfolk, 1647. British Museum Dept of Prints and Drawings BMC680 18 May 1647, reproduced by permission of the Trustees.

Witches

What sort of people were identified as witches? Briggs and Coward both suggest that most witches had a long-standing reputation, were involved in some breach of neighbourliness and were often people regarded as outsiders to the community – often women.

Exercise   Turn now to the *Anthology* (II.30 and 31) and answer the following questions:

1   What kind of evidence is presented?

2   What do these documents tell us about relations within the communities?

Discussion   1   Notice that much of the evidence is hearsay. The testimony of what people had said to one another about a third party was permitted. Marie Nicaise reported both what her late husband had said and what the priest said. John Rivet reported what he had been told about the women living near him. Matthew Hopkins reported what Elizabeth Clarke said to him and Elizabeth Clarke reported various things said to her by Anne West.

2   There are elements of both affairs which seem to be storms in teacups and we learn more about relations between individuals than about relations within the community. Reputation was obviously very significant. It was important for those who had a good reputation to keep it, but equally there seem to have been people who had long-standing reputations as witches, long before there was any question of prosecution. Elizabeth Clarke had even had relations who had been executed as witches. Marie Lanenchin was well known as a witch and she was in the position of a supplicant whose request was refused. Elizabeth Clarke was pitied by Anne West. Poverty and minute social gradations also play their part in these accounts. Note, too, that John Rivet is quite happy to acknowledge that he had sought the help of a cunning woman to cure his wife by charms.

Witchcraft and the local community

What does all this tell us about relations in local communities? It certainly tells us about the mixture of beliefs within communities and the tensions that might exist there. All the countries shared a common Christian culture and its inversion by the invocation of evil, though black magic rites involving use of the host (consecrated bread) and holy words were not common to all countries. Many of the confessions exacted from people accused of witchcraft seem to be sincere, that is the confessor believed that she (as it usually was) had actually done the things that had been claimed for her. Ireland had the least incidence of witchcraft prosecutions (and the only trial for which there is actual evidence, that of Florence Newton of Youghal, co. Cork in 1661, took place purely within the English Protestant community). One of the reasons for this may be that of all our countries, it was the one which had preserved more pre-Christian and non-mainline Christian practices amongst the population at large. Irish Catholicism was noted by the papacy for preserving many features of much older practices.

During our period the impact of the Protestant and Catholic reformations began to reach much more distant districts. The clergy defined orthodoxy much more closely than had the medieval church. Seventeenth-century political élites required a greater conformity from their subjects for which the church provided the ideological weapons. Mountainous and remote regions which had not previously been part of a national church organization found themselves with churches and ministers. In the Jura, the mountainous region in the south east of France on the borders of Switzerland, almost every village was reputed to have a witch and the term *hérége* (heretic) was used to mean witch rather than the usual French term *sorcière*. In north-western France, on the border with the Spanish Netherlands, there were highly localized outbreaks of witch hunting, as there were in Lorraine. These border regions were not part of the kingdom of France in the early seventeenth century and only came under its central government after the wars of Louis XIV. On the other hand there was also witchcraft in and around Paris and in Languedoc (central southern France).

In Scotland the establishment of kirk sessions in each parish brought much more of the population within reach of moral supervision. The kirk sessions dealt with minor crimes and matters of morality. They also controlled geographical migration. It is most striking that the lowest incidence of witchcraft (as revealed in the official record) was in the Gaelic-speaking Western Highlands and the Western Isles where the parish organization was least effective. The connection between religion and the prosecution of witchcraft in Scotland is absolutely explicit in the formula of the accusation:

> It is of verity that you the said — having shaken off all fear of God and reverence and regard of the divine ordinance, laws and acts of parliament of this kingdom ...

This connection between the law, secular and divine, was a particularly important part of the Scottish polity in the seventeenth century. The ideal of the godly state informed government policy and the secular law was used to impose the divine will.

With the spread of a more uniform religion came a more uniform system of justice. Monarchs made extensive efforts to establish royal courts of justice to replace those which had been operated by their noble feudal tenants. Throughout France, England, Wales and Scotland ancient jurisdictions were abolished and replaced by royal courts. These courts were concerned with using the power of the state to regulate social tensions. The introduction of prosecutors in France and Scotland extended the process. This happened in different ways in the two countries, but its effect was that royal or judicial officials became responsible for initiating prosecutions. Until then, all prosecutions resulted from personal complaints made by members of the community who considered themselves, their families or their property to have been harmed by the alleged witch. Prosecutors came from a group noted for its scepticism about witchcraft.

Attempts to link increased incidences of witchcraft prosecutions with general social or economic conditions have not been very successful.

Local conditions do seem to have played an important part, especially those which led to community tensions. Pressures *internal* to the community seem to have led to a rise in prosecutions rather than pressures *external* to it. Thus a local shortage of land or resources might have a more marked effect than a widespread war.

Finally, how do we account for the fact that the majority of prosecutions were against women, though their predominance varied in different parts of Europe and within individual countries? Mere misogyny is too general an explanation for something which produced specific accusations against named people, so too is the idea of unease at the breaking down of the old order. I am inclined to feel that the issue of authority, especially female authority is involved, but why did it become such an issue in the sixteenth and seventeenth centuries?

Conclusion

In this unit we have seen something of how local communities regulated themselves, yet at the same time interacted with other communities and with the state. In France, England and Wales the local government of these communities seems to have been drawn from an increasingly narrow range of people, becoming more oligarchic and more subject to control from the centre. How far the decline in witchcraft prosecutions was a consequence of greater control and how far it was a part of a more widespread change in sensibilities is difficult to estimate. But changes in provision for the poor meant that they were regulated to a much greater extent. Perhaps the opportunities for marginal people to lead independent existences were reduced as well. Scotland and Ireland remained much less governed than France, England and Wales. In both countries communities were much affected by the fact that there were substantial proportions of the sparsely distributed and remotely situated population who were at odds with the official religion or government of the country. But we still await good local studies of communities in all these countries to understand better the diversity between them.

References

Foucault, M. (1961), *Folie et deraison: Histoire de la Folie à l'âge classique*, Plon, Paris.

Gough, R. (1981), *The History of Myddle*, edited by David Hey, Penguin, Harmondsworth.

Gutton, J-P. (1974), *La Sociabilité Villageois dans l'Ancienne France*, Hachette, Paris.

Jordan, W.K. (1962), *The Social Institutions of Lancashire: a Study of the Changing Pattern of Aspirations in Lancashire 1480–1660*, Chetham Society, Manchester.

Petit, A. and Mathieu, G. (1911), *Inventaire Sommaire des Archives Hospitalières anterieur à 1790: Hôpitaux de Tulle, Brive, Ussel, Argentat, Treignac, Meymac, Tulle*, Tulle.

Slack, P. (1988), *Poverty and Policy in Tudor and Stuart England*, Longman, London.

Unit 10
The household in the seventeenth century

Prepared for the course team by Rosemary O'Day

Contents

Study timetable

Weeks of study	Texts	Video	AC	Set books
2	Unit 10; *Anthology*, II. 32–35; Illustration Book	Video 10		Coward, Briggs

Objectives

By the end of this unit you should be able to:

1   appreciate the view of some contemporaries that the power of the father/husband figure in the household was absolute. This was an important premise in the thought of some of those who sought justification for the absolute power of the monarch in the state, whose work will be given further consideration in Unit 13;

2   appreciate that this view was not held by everyone and, moreover, that even those who did declare such a view might still reserve important roles within the family for members other than the head;

3   appreciate the methodological problems involved in deciding how much influence church and state had upon the seventeenth-century household;

4   have some real understanding of the variety of household forms and what this meant for any idea that the state might exercise effective social control through the heads of households.

Introduction

By the beginning of the seventeenth century England, Scotland and France had a long tradition of debate about the appropriateness of female rule which had developed against the background of female claims to the succession or to the regency (Mary Stuart in Scotland; Mary Tudor and Elizabeth I in England; Catherine de Medici in France). A salic law operated in France which denied the succession to females; no such law existed in England or Scotland. Opponents of female rule saw the accession of a woman as unnatural, against the law and against scripture. Its proponents argued that to rule a woman had to renounce her private person and don the public persona, effectively, of a man. In the last quarter of the sixteenth century the French jurist Jean Bodin introduced into the arena an argument for male rule which was to provide the motif for seventeenth-century debates not about the permissibility of female rule but the nature of monarchical power in the kingdom. The state, he wrote, was like a household and it replicated the organization of that household. Just as the husband and father had authority and power over all members of the household, so in the state the monarch, the father of his people, had this authority and power. James I used the same metaphor. 'I am the Husband, and the whole Isle is my lawful wife.' 'A King is trewly *Parens patriae*, the politique father of his people.' (See Unit 13.) Sir Robert Filmer, who used the scriptures as a source book for his political theory, argued that kings, like ordinary fathers, derived their absolute authority from the God-given fatherly authority of Adam.

These arguments for the monarch's replication of the patriarchal power and authority of the father could, as this tradition suggests, be used to oppose the rule of women and to support the absolute authority of the monarch (father) over all his subjects (children). With respect to the rule of women such arguments would, as Unit 13 makes clear, be particularly relevant to the France of the Frondes (during the regency of Anne of Austria) and the England and Wales of the later Stuarts (Mary II and Anne). With regard to the authority of the king over his subjects they had a special relevance to the period preceding and during the English civil wars.

What was this household to which contemporaries likened the state? In seventeenth- and eighteenth-century France, England, Wales, Scotland and the English-settled parts of Ireland, scholars have identified the primary social unit as the household. The family, which might or might not be co-resident and which was a kinship concept, was not co-terminous with the household. For example, children did not cease to belong to the family when they left home but they did cease to be members of a household. In this unit we shall concern ourselves only with the institution of the household which was, at some stage in its cycle, based upon one or more families of parents and children and their servants.

This was the household to which contemporary theorists referred when they likened the state to the household and the king to the father. Part of the purpose of this unit is to see how far this idea of the household tallied with actual household structure and organization.

The household

The composition and structure of households in this period is a contentious issue among historians. Until recently most subscribed to the idea of a European marriage pattern, characterized for most of the population by late age at marriage and small numbers of children. Historical demographers have described a western European society in which households were also small. They believed that, with very few exceptions amongst the élite, households contained one conjugal unit of parents and children (known as a simple nuclear family), along with house and field servants and apprentices. This is the 'household' described in most of the textbooks (including Coward, pp.39–40) and so it is important that you should be conversant with it and with the terms commonly used to describe it. This is a description which is, however, under considerable revision. Historians now suggest a much wider variation in household form, size and organization. Later on in this unit, I shall return to this issue of the composition and organization of households.

Church and state displayed tremendous interest in the 'family' – a term which they often used interchangeably with 'household'. Why? The household was potentially extremely useful as an organ of social control and economic stability: it could supervise closely its junior members; it might channel the energies of the economically productive and physically strong members of the biological family into providing for, and caring for, weak offspring and elderly kin. Biology provided the clue to the strength of the family unit: it was because people had a natural affection for their close relatives that they were willing and able to support one another economically. State, community and church were eager to exploit this family commitment. The church was essentially interested in the individual soul; the state was not so much interested in the individual as in the strength of the nation. Jean Bodin had written in 1576, 'When families are well governed, so will the commonwealth be well governed' (cited in Pillorget, 1991, p.13). The English writer William Gouge (1622) said something similar: 'Necessary it is that good order be first set in families: for as they were before polities, so they are somewhat the more necessary: and good members of the family are like to make good members of Church and Commonwealth'. Recently it has been suggested that in France there was a Family–State Compact that was designed to bring family formation under parental (i.e. patriarchal) control in the first instance, and under the magisterial control of the Paris *parlement* in the second, and that regulated family matters (i.e. marriage regulations, reproductive customs, inheritance rules, and marital separation arrangements) to this end.

Marriage

In France, children who resisted their father's marriage choices could be imprisoned, daughters for longer periods than sons. In cases where a daughter of less than 25 years married without her parents' permission, the groom was liable to the death penalty and the marriage was declared clandestine. Moves towards such a compact might also be identified in England although its success in both cases is uncertain. In England, the insistence by the church that mutual consent of both parties was essential to a valid marriage, irrespective of parental consent, acted against the power of parents to force their children into marriages and supported the actions of those children who entered into unions without their parents' express agreement. In France, secular law disregarded the church's position. In practice, in both England and France, open revolt against parental authority was rare and, when it did take place, parents usually gave belated consent.

Seventeenth-century men and women, however, saw marriage as more than the union of two individuals for the purpose of reproduction and companionship. Marriage was about the formation of economically viable households; it was about forming and cementing political and economic connections at the national, regional and local levels. The making of marriage was, therefore, seen by grandparents, parents and children as a family affair. In 1634 Gaston d'Orléans, brother of Louis XIII and heir presumptive to the French throne, underwent a clandestine marriage to Marguerite of Lorraine. Mathieu Molé, *procureur général* of the Paris *parlement*, declared during discussions that 'marriages are brought about, not for the pleasure of the persons who enter into the contract, but for the honour and advantage of their families' (Molé, 1855–7, p.227). What applied to a royal family, applied to the families of bourgeoisie and peasantry. A people raised to see marriage in this light were less liable to resist its making by others than might be supposed by students of history reared in a different tradition.

The dependence of children upon their parents and guardians provided an additional inducement to many to defer to their authority. A power relationship between parents and children was, if you like, encouraged by economic factors.

At this point I would like you to read Coward, pp.50–8 and Briggs, pp.44–5. This reading pinpoints a major distinction between French and English rural society at this time. France had an independent peasantry whereas England did not. It also highlights the precariousness of life in both countries and the importance of the successful organization of the household to survival.

The seventeenth-century economy, which was dominated by farming the land, made children extremely dependent upon the good will of their parents. In England children could marry before the death of the father but it was none the less true that children of both sexes found it much easier to make a satisfactory livelihood with continued parental support or an inheritance. In northern Europe the male came of age when he became independent and this independence was commonly marked by the founding of a family, the formation of a separate household or 'economic unit'. In parts of peasant France it was marriage that secured emancipation from the father's absolute control and it was, as we shall see later, only the father who could enter into the binding contract that was marriage. It was unthinkable that a separate household should be created without the wherewithal to support it and marriage without means was deplored.

In most social classes in England and northern France marriage was associated with maturity. The legal age for marriage might have been low (in England it was 12 for girls and 14 for boys) but the actual age at marriage for most of the population was high (in early seventeenth-century England the average for grooms was between 27 and 29 and for brides

26) and rising throughout the period. Normally only the rich married young and, when they did so, they frequently did not set up independent households or even cohabit. Child marriages amongst the English élite were on the decrease. For the middling sort every possible obstacle was placed in the way of early marriage and household formation. The statutory age of the termination of apprenticeships in England, for example, stood at 24. The tendency of young migrants to the cities to marry early was deplored. In France, impediments to early marriage were generally respected until the early eighteenth century. By then, however, more people were entering into marriage without the necessary material support and the number of legitimate children being abandoned increased as a consequence. The practical obstacles in the way of premature independence were reinforced by contemporary teaching.

In a course designed to demonstrate the development of the state and the relationship of the governors to the governed within it, the whole notion of dependence and independence is of enormous importance. Within the household the economically dependent were denied other forms of independence. At a time when wages were low, many young people had to wait a long time before they could afford to marry.

Sometimes the local economy, the structure of the household and the prevalent inheritance patterns discouraged early marriage and made the single life the lot of many. In parts of the south of France, for example, it was not the practice of younger sons to marry from the house of the parents or, indeed, to acquire sufficient property to support an independent household once the parents were dead. This was especially true of the south west (the Pyrenees in particular) where mother, father, eldest son and his wife and children tended to live together in what has come to be called a stem family. In this stem family household might also co-reside unmarried siblings of the eldest son. Probably as a consequence of this practice, there were large numbers of bachelors in this region. In some other parts of the south west marriage took place at a much younger age than in the rest of France. In these areas – the present Charente-Maritime, Dordogne and Haute-Viennes – the extended family household permitted younger children to marry and continue to live with their parents. (Textbooks sometimes describe such an extended family as the patriarchal family.)

Exercise   What are we observing here about family relationships?

Discussion You would probably have noted that, as they were dependent upon their parents both for preparation for independence and for support thereafter, children were, generally speaking, willing to conform to the unwritten and written rules for their survival. These rules appear to have varied from country to country, region to region, and town to countryside.

You may also have noted that the more we discover about the variety of household (and family) forms, the more shaky appears the suggestion that most households in these societies were based on the simple nuclear family.

Inheritance

The rules of inheritance might reinforce such varied patterns. For example, under the custom of Irish gavelkind, land belonged to the sept (or clan) and family property was in the form of cattle divided between the children. In peasant France property belonged to the family. There were birth rights in the family land. Land could not be sold unless the children were first offered it at a reasonable price (*restrait lignager*). Inherited property belonged to the descent group and even the transmission of acquired property was hedged in with rules to protect this group. Marriage contracts and wills were used to spell out the descent of property but for the majority who died intestate, in the absence of a carefully worded marriage contract, inheritance was governed by the various customs. In much of France the custom favoured equal partible inheritance. For example, in Bordeaux, where a male died intestate, unless the marriage contract stated otherwise, his property of whatever type would be divided equally between his heirs. Even if he made a will, the custom dictated that he must leave all his inherited property to his direct descendants or, if he had no heirs, give two-thirds to his nearest blood (consanguine) kin. He was allowed to favour one child over the others but not to their total exclusion. Property that had been acquired by him could be freely willed away only if he were celibate or had a childless marriage; if there were direct heirs of the marriage they would inherit the acquired property (*acquets*). A study of wills has shown that parents of both sexes used the opportunity to provide for all their children, with fathers showing a slight preference in bequests for their sons and mothers for their daughters. In parts of southern France, however, the patrimony was passed to one child although not necessarily to the eldest son. Other children received only a legitimate portion of disposable goods and chattels.

In England and Wales, freehold, copyhold and leasehold land were held not by the family but by the individual. Children, even the eldest son, had no rights in the land from birth and specific pieces of property could be willed as the testator wished unless he or she had bound themselves legally by contract to act otherwise. The rights of the firstborn son (or the co-heiresses in the absence of a son) to a third of freehold land and of a widow to her portion were safeguarded by the Statute of Wills (1540). The testator could specify which portions of land were bestowed on the heir or widow. But most land was held not freehold but by leasehold or copyhold or as part of a trust. Those holding land according to these other forms of tenure had absolute freedom of testation, saving only the widow's dower, although what individuals did with their property was to some extent governed by custom.

In the courts which determined the validity of wills and administered the distribution of property in cases of intestacy, ancient custom (such as that of *legitim* described below) guided practice. In the absence of a will, under common law, unless the landowner took measures to the contrary, real property passed on death to the eldest son or, failing a male heir, to the daughters. Where there was a will, one-third of the freehold estate was reserved to the heir. In areas where partible inheritance or, more occasionally, ultimogeniture pertained, such land passed instead either to all the children or to the youngest. Contracts and settlements made to protect the property and other rights of married women were not recognized by the common law courts but could be, and were, defended under the equitable jurisdiction of Chancery. Bequests of moveable property, such as money or possessions, seem on occasion to have obeyed ancient customs but were in fact freely bequeathed. Such bequests were often funded by the sale of real property by the executors. These rules of inheritance perhaps made children in England and Wales even keener to stay in their parents' good books. But exclusion from a will seems to have been more threatened than executed.

Exercise Read the following short extracts. What conclusions do you think they point to concerning family strategies in making bequests?

1 Brother, I may have often occasion to alter the porcons of money given to my sister's children. (Lichfield Joint Record Office, Will of John Hill, Rector of Elford, proved 16 January 1621/2)

2 [The executor should administer the estate] to the benefit of [his] children' and 'that more especial regard by him be taken of the weaker sort of my sayd children for that some of them (god be thanked) are well enabled with strength and competent gifts to get their own livings and to be an aid and stay to their weaker brethren. (Lichfield Joint Record Office, proved 1 December 1618)

3 ... acknowledging all too little to recompence the portion she brought me in marriage and the love and care she hath expres'd towards me ever since [my wife shall have half of the estate to dispose of on death] at her will. (Lichfield Joint Record Office, Will of Matthew Fowler, Rector of Whitechurch, Salop, proved 3 March 1683/4)

Discussion 1 This indicates that this testator was aware of his own changing circumstances and prepared to adjust his bequests to accommodate these as well as perhaps the changing relationship with and needs of these nephews and nieces as they grew older. It might also suggest that the testator had no children of his own when he made the will.

2 This extract shows that this testator was anxious to provide for his children according to their perceived needs and did not give priority to the eldest son. Indeed the stated assumption is that the stronger will care for the weaker. He wanted his executor to know what was in his mind and administer the estate accordingly.

3 This shows the testator making a generous settlement to his wife not 'as of right' but because she had been a good wife and also had brought a generous settlement on marriage. There was no direct relationship between the dowry (the portion which the wife brought to her husband) and the dower (the part of the estate bequeathed to the widow). He makes no stipulation that she will lose this share of the estate if she remarries (we have no idea how old this couple were). On her own death she will be able to dispose of her half share of the estate freely – it will not revert, as in many cases it did, to the direct heirs of the body.

It is worth noting that the custom of *legitim*, whereby a widow without off-spring inherited one-half of her husband's moveable goods (including leasehold land) after his debts had been paid, and a widow with offspring one-third, had ceased to be enforced in the Province of Canterbury by the late sixteenth century although it was still observed in the North until the 1690s and may have served as a rule of thumb when testators every-where drew up their wills. The demise of the custom led to longer and more detailed wills, on the one hand, and perhaps to increased use of the marriage settlement, whereby the property of the wife was protected for her widowhood by a contract defensible in the court of Chancery. Recent work suggests that perhaps as many as 10 per cent of the probate accounts of married testators (whatever their social origins) in the seven-teenth and early eighteenth centuries reveal the existence of such mar-riage settlements.

Studies of family strategy in England suggest that parents from both the élite and the middling sort were concerned first and foremost to pro-tect the future livelihood of all of their children, not simply the eldest and certainly not just the males, and, that assured, the interests of a sur-viving spouse. Treatment of a widow was not penal but prudential: as long as she remained part of the husband's household she was provided for but if she remarried and formed a new household this provision normally ceased.

The attitude of state and church to the household

Exercise On the basis of the above material does it appear to you that the family was the creation of the church or the state?

Discussion The family in early modern France and England and Wales (and else-where) evolved in response to a number of influences amongst which the prescriptions of church and state were but two. There was a natural inclination among parents to care for their children during their immaturity and to provide for their future independence. The manner in which these functions were organized within a household responded to customary, traditional, legal and economic influences.

Both state and church favoured a model of the family that consciously mimicked the patriarchal family household of the Old Testament, modi-fied in certain respects by New Testament example and teaching. Essen-tially the example was that of the Holy Family of Mary, Joseph and Jesus and the teaching that of Paul of Tarsus. Early modern teaching empha-sized the co-resident nuclear family of parents and children and the household in which they lived together, that included servants. For a number of reasons, therefore, this was a very restricted concept of 'family' and, indeed, the household.

It may be interesting to note what the reasons might be. Here are some suggestions:

- scriptural precept;
- preference – the word of God declared that this was how Christians should organize their lives. It was not to the state's advantage to nurture more extensive concepts of family – the interest group created by close-knit but far-flung networks of near and distant kin was to be feared not encouraged; the church was interested in the salvation of the individual and the relatively small nuclear family encompassing the natural relationships of authority-respect, concern-clinging, discipline-obedience between parents and their children was perceived as an excellent vehicle to bring individuals to the church;
- custom – contemporaries assumed that the organization in which they themselves had been raised was not only normal but unquestionable. (It is, however, true that many contemporaries did not live in what might be termed simple nuclear families. I shall return to this point shortly.)

Forms of household organization

If we read contemporary texts prescribing how family life should be lived we could, therefore, be forgiven for concluding that the people of the time lived in small nuclear family households with their servants and that the wider sense of family – that of continuing links with previously co-resident siblings or children and also that of the even more extensive kin group – was unimportant. But was this the case?

There is no space here to discuss the extent to which contemporaries nurtured these wider senses of 'family'. But there were alternative forms of household organization in seventeenth- and early eighteenth-century Britain and Europe that find no mention in contemporary works of theory and yet were of importance. Laslett (1972, 1983), committed to the view that northern European households were small (a mean size of 4.75 including domestic servants), agrees that over a third of households might be described as 'large'.

Other scholars have demonstrated that the household had a cycle of its own. A household began when a couple married (size: 2 persons). Then it grew when they had children (size: 3+). It reduced in size when the children left home (size 2). In an age when residential servant-keeping was common and widespread throughout the upper and middling social groups, the size of the household would be increased by the complement of such servants especially during the infancy and childhood of offspring when the need for additional labour was high.

There might be variations on this theme. For example, a widowed mother might co-reside with married son and his wife and children or a young couple might live with the parents of one partner before setting up an independent household. (In eighteenth-century Haute Provence more than a third of marriage contracts envisaged the young couple living with the parents of one of them. In England and Wales élite families often

Figure 26
Louis Le Nain, La Famille
Heureuse, dit le retour du
Baptême, The Happy
Family, named the return
from the Baptism, *1642, oil
on canvas, 61 x 78 cm.
Louvre, Donation Paul Jamot.
Photo: Réunion des Musées
Nationaux Documentation
Photographique.*

anticipated that a young couple would live in the family of origin of one
or other spouse at least for a brief period.)

But not all households were based on the simple nuclear family's
cycle. Study of a village in Finistère revealed, especially among the relatively prosperous farmers, large numbers of complex households where
three generations of a family lived together. This pattern had persisted
since at least the sixteenth century. Where egalitarian partible inheritance was the custom, there were fewer complex households than where
other customs prevailed. When there were large numbers of complex
households, even when they did not form a majority of units, they sometimes contained a higher percentage of the total population than 'normal' nuclear households.

There were other forms of complex household that diverged more
markedly from the upwardly or downwardly extended nuclear family. For
instance, in areas such as the southern Alps, Gascony and Limousin dou-
ble households in which lived two married couples, each with their offspring, and occasionally an unmarried brother or sister who worked for
their keep were common. In such cases the family was closely identified
with property and a house that was regarded as inalienable and indivis-
ible. Joint households of this type tended to belong to peasantry of at
least average wealth. The head of the household selected an heir (normally from among his children and usually but not inevitably the eldest
son) who lived in the household, brought his wife there, raised his family
there and worked there until such time as he came into his inheritance.
The simple nuclear household was characteristic of the poorer peasants
in the same area who had no estate to hand down. Large complex family
groups were also common in the livestock rearing areas in the centre of
France. Down to the mid-eighteenth century more than two-thirds of the

parishioners of La Courtine dwelt in households containing at least two conjugal units (i.e. married couples with their minor children), surviving unmarried adult offspring and a number of young children.

The dowry paid to the head of the household with the heir's bride was used to buy out the interest in the estate of any unmarried sons. Probably such households were common throughout France in earlier times but they seem to have more or less disappeared in northern France by the seventeenth century, persisting largely in central, western and southern regions. Elsewhere in France, in the Nivernais province, the Bourbonnais and parts of Limousin and Berry, even more complex family communities, including households of married brothers (*frérèches*), occurred. Households of between 12 and 30 individuals, all related, formed a *commaunité taisible* and shared a large farm and house. Everything was communally held. The men elected one of their number as household head and he acted to sign leases and marriage contracts. If anybody wished to leave such a community they did so but could take with them only their personal belongings and a few coins. Complex households may have been less usual in England and Wales but they did exist.

There were other forms of household complexity that are hidden by statistics. The percentage of marriages in England and Wales which were second or third marriages only gradually decreased from its high of 30 per cent during the seventeenth century. In northern France in the early eighteenth century 30 per cent of marriages still involved widows or widowers. Those who had been widowed, therefore, made a considerable contribution to complex family forms in the period. What looks like a simple nuclear family in a household listing might in reality have been a very complex nuclear-type family containing step-parents and step-children. Chaytor (1980) describes the enormous and changing complexity of the 'French' household in Ryton in the late sixteenth and early seventeenth century: at one time it contained two married couples and five young children from various marriages yet at other times it consisted of a single nuclear family of husband, wife and children. We call these hybrid complex families.

Exercise   Based on your reading so far what do you think were the implications of the above for the model of the family offered by the church and the state?

Discussion   You may think that the model offered bore little resemblance to reality for quite considerable numbers.

Authority relations

The existence of complex households posed problems of authority relations when compared to the simple model proposed. You may not know the answers, but did well if you considered questions such as these when two or more couples (and their children) lived together, who had authority within the household? Who managed the farm? Who controlled the children? Who decided what was to be done and by whom in the house itself and on the part of the farm that was seen as the wife's preserve in both England and Wales and northern France when there were two or more wives?

Historians don't know the answer. Certainly we know that the *communités* customarily elected a household head. In some complex English households such as the Ferrar household at Little Gidding there is a suggestion that the component nuclear families actually dwelt in separate domiciles although the 'household' concept prevailed when decisions relating to the whole family economy and society were concerned. Architectural plans of *frèrèche* farmhouses in the Jura indicate that the families of brothers farmed together and technically lived in the same house but preserved a separation between their families' sleeping and living quarters. But these examples provide only occasional glimpses into a complex and largely hidden family landscape.

Exercise Turn now to *Anthology*, II. 32. What does this extract tell us about the location of authority in the household.

Discussion As far as housekeeping was concerned, authority lay with a woman – in 1691 with Josias's widowed elderly mother; after 1709 with his wife, Sybill (who had previously kept house for her own father).

When Widow Stout grew too infirm to keep house for her middle-aged bachelor son he had alternative courses of action – to keep house with a servant or to take a wife. Note that the option of keeping house for himself was not considered. When he took a wife he appears to have required or at least sought his mother's approval despite his age (48).

The addition of another adult woman to the household occasioned conflict. Both women were strong minded and both wished to housekeep. A resolution of this conflict, which became unbearable after a year, was sought and found by Josias. He asked his younger brother, William, to take their mother and appears to have paid towards her future upkeep.

Josias was a man who liked a domestic peace. For this reason he allowed his strong-willed wife her way.

The example shows both the potential severity of the problem when a widow and a daughter-in-law lived in the same house and the manner in which this was negotiated not only by the parties concerned but by the wider group of non-co-resident offspring. For authority depended upon personality and habit as much as upon the legal position.

It does seem that there was a potentially more acute problem of authority in hybrid complex families than in simple nuclear families and that contemporary theorists did not address these problems except in the most cursory way. Dod and Cleaver's popular *A Godly Forme of Household Government* counselled readers who were twice married not to speak overmuch of a former partner to the new to avoid irritation and aggravation and to treat step-children with love as *in loco parentis*. Legal arrangements were frequently made to avoid authority contests in the case of hybrid families but friction was seemingly sufficiently frequent as to result in step-children leaving home early on a permanent basis.

Now we need to consider how might we sum up the match or mismatch between the theory and the practice of household authority relations.

Church and state favoured a simple form of domestic organization – a household – that reduced the problem of authority relations to those between husband and wife, parents and children, master and mistress and servants. They had a biblical blueprint for such a family and, insofar as they could, they sought to impose it upon society. This model did not represent reality for quite large numbers of the population. We need to find strategies to reveal whether the power relations which prevailed were oppressive and whether they were different in kind from those sketched by those in authority in church and state.

To do this we might:

1   try to balance the prescriptive with the descriptive by examining actual families as they lived;

2   try to examine more closely the printed and manuscript prescriptive literature and other forms of literature (for example, ballads, chapbooks, contemporary poetry and drama) for clues about the marriage relationship.

Examining families

The attempt to describe the lives of households in the past is bedevilled by the nature of the historian's evidence. We have a good deal of information about a few families, usually from the upper and upper middle echelons of society and derived from private correspondence, diaries and autobiographies, and very little about most households. The evidence for England is far superior to that for the other societies under discussion. Historians would like to draw a distinction, where appropriate, between the households in, for example, urban and rural areas and in different types of rural community. They would like to be able to chart chronological change against this backdrop. While we would like to discover the experience of household relations throughout society, our evidence does not permit this. The most that we can do is paint a general picture of these relations, in the hope and expectation that future evidence will either confirm or contest it.

Peasant French men and women worked in partnership on the farm. It has become fashionable to compartmentalize the work of men and women in our minds. Men worked in the fields; women worked in the house. We should, however, beware of this approach. There was no rigid compartmentalization of life between domestic activities and the work of production. Women lit the fires, fetched the water, did the cooking, washed the clothes, made preserves, swept, dusted, made the beds, knit and sewed, cared for the children and managed the farmyard and garden. The garden provided food for the household and the farm animals – cabbages and other vegetables and, in the farmyard, poultry, eggs, milk, cheese, butter and pig swill. It required daily and arduous labour. Men chopped the wood, prepared the soil, tended the vines, managed the cows and horses, and on winter evenings made baskets and did repair work around the house and farm. But there was a complementarity about the work of man and woman on the farm. The man chopped the wood, the woman laid and lit the fire. And there was also a certain interchangeability and co-operation. Both men and women made bread. In some places the wife managed as well as milked the cows, in others the duties were split. In yet others it was men who took the cows to their summer pastures and who made the butter and cheese. In the fields, the man might lead the oxen and the women guide the plough harnessed to them. Men and women shared in the work of harvest, bringing in the cereal crops, picking and treading the grapes. Men tended to handle the heavier implements leaving the lighter sickle to the women. In the winter both men and women were more confined to the house and to the men fell more of the work associated with food preparation.

The similarities are striking in England and here we have superior seventeenth- and early eighteenth-century evidence to indicate that the description holds true for the period as a whole. The wife of a late seventeenth-century dissenting minister kept a herd of kine (cows) to supplement her husband's income as minister and school teacher. Another young wife sold cabbages from her cottage garden.

There is a good deal of evidence to suggest that the roles of both husbands and wives varied, as we might expect, in relation to the degree of prosperity. For a well-born woman, the tasks were set against a background of considerably more leisure and were perhaps largely managerial in nature. But even women from the upper and upper middle classes wound yarn, organized meals, made preserves, embroidered wall hangings, kept the books and saw to the household's medical and other needs. A study of women's diaries in the Stuart period suggests that there were 'fewer class variations in women's daily round of activities than might have been expected' (Mendelson, 1985, p.190). Wives' participation in public life tended to complement that of their husbands. Well-born women seem to have played an important part in offering health care and hospitality in the locality. Midwifery for family members and neighbourhood fell to both married and unmarried women. Even female, unmarried, servants had their hierarchy. In the Gévaudan, female servants were ranged under the *maitresse servante*, whose role was organizational.

Within the urban environment there was also traditionally a complementarity between the work of husbands and wives. Whether they acted beyond male control or not and whether or not they were discriminated against, women were very much involved in both rural and urban economic life as farmers and linen merchants, laundry women and nurses, servants and property owners, money lenders and creditors as well as beggars and prostitutes. The regulatory mechanisms of the state and the municipality in both France and England simply made them more invisible than they had been. Moreover, it was expected of them that they should be involved even when the assumption was that the husband or other male kin were in control.

Marriage was regarded as and ideally lived as a partnership – this partnership was dedicated to procreation and rearing the children. Each person had their own role in family, neighbourhood and polity. These roles involved relationships: a man might be husband to a wife, father to a child (and as a consequence relatively powerful); in the church be a child of God; in the workplace a journeyman or servant; and in the state a subject.

The power of the father over the children was clearly defined within French law. Although Jean Bodin's plea that fathers be allowed power of life and death over their children was not satisfied, fathers maintained absolute control in other respects. Children could not enter binding contracts (such as loans or marriages) nor make wills (even with a father's consent) because they had no absolute right to property, even over their own persons. In those French provinces where the written law ran, these rules applied unless the father formally emancipated his children or they achieved exalted public positions. Elsewhere, where the law was customary, their applicability was variable. It was not, however, in either England and Wales or France, up to the father to choose a child's future occupation. This was God's prerogative. Then it was the parents' duty to see that a child was prepared for the estate to which God had called him or her. It was in this context that contemporaries made the educational provision outlined in Unit 6. We should not overemphasize the strength of patriarchy within this French family, however, for envisaging the father as an independent, free-acting individual is a mistake. The reverse side of the inability of the children to make contracts and wills was that the father himself could not alienate property because it belonged to the family.

In England and Wales, the father's control over his children was a matter of precept and pragmatism rather than law. He had the power of the purse, the power of property, the power of precept. A child could easily be left penniless should the father make a will to that effect, subject to the reservations mentioned earlier (see p.127). A child had no birthright.

None the less the assumption in both countries was that the children would inherit. Fatherhood was not power for its own sake, it was power in the interests of the household and family and its survival.

Historians have often fixed upon the issue of arranged marriages to demonstrate the power of the father over children during the early modern period. In theory there is a distinction between an arranged marriage (where the parents selected the spouse for their child) and a marriage where parental consent was required. In practice, the distinction is often blurred. A marriage might be 'arranged' within a context of wide consultation and concern. Children might form hopes of particular marriages but accept that parental input and consent was important. Examination of the making of marriages indicates that children generally deferred to their parents when marriage became an issue. This was true even when the children were in fact adults who did not require parental consent. Look back to Josias Stout (*Anthology*, II. 32) who was 48 when he sought his mother's permission before he married.

Common sense told the couple that life would be much easier in every way if the parents gave consent. But it was not only the father or head of household who was involved. If anything, mothers and grandmothers played as large or a larger part than male relatives in arranging marriages. There is every suggestion that the interests and preferences of the young people involved were uppermost in the minds of the adults and indeed were actively consulted. Parents acted in accordance with various criteria, prominent amongst which were the economic viability of the marriage, the compatibility of the couple in terms of personality and emotional make up as well as sexual performance, and the extent to which the liaison would protect kin links and provide for the surviving spouse in the event of the death of one spouse.

Among the French peasantry there is the suggestion that marriage was very much a family affair – it represented the continuation of the household on the father's death. Young people themselves also used these same criteria. Founding or continuing an independent household was a serious business for all concerned. Young people lower down the social scale met with less active involvement from their parents and families probably because the question of an 'independent household' was not at issue. There are plenty of examples of conflict within the family, when sons and daughters struggled to secure a match that their parents refused to countenance and when parents used heavy-handed tactics to ensure that they were obeyed. But this scenario was neither normal nor considered desirable either in France or England and Wales. Our understanding of how marriages were made is helped if we reject the ideas of 'arrangement' and 'veto' in favour of a system of consultation and consensus which was on occasion riven by conflict.

Servants

In these countries servant-keeping was common. Contemporary literature laid down ground rules for the relationship between masters and mistresses and their servants. The master and mistress were to act *in loco parentis*. It was to be a caring and non-exploitative relationship. Servants were to regard their masters and mistresses as if they were their parents. They were to look after their interests as if these were their parents. But in practice there was love between father and mother and children and this could not be created between master and mistress and servants. There was no suggestion that any one should try.

The enormous variety of different types of servant almost defies description. In some parts of society it was common for parents to send adolescent children into another home for a period of 'service'. Sometimes these children went to the household of a relative of similar social standing or higher. But not all servants were youngsters. Some had long service in one household, others moved from place to place so often that they could scarcely have been regarded as 'children of the household'. Nevertheless contemporaries at all social levels insisted that children and servants were different in kind.

In 1644 the Essex clergyman, Ralph Josselin, welcomed his 21 year-old spinster sister Mary into his household 'as servant'. He had to remind himself that she was his sister and that because of this biological relationship she would not be treated as a servant. 'My respect is and shall be towards her as a sister.' Few servants deluded themselves. At around the same time Adam Martindale, a private tutor to unruly boys, was exploited by his master and, with his master's connivance, by the boys themselves.

Servant abuse, including sexual abuse, is a recurrent theme in both societies. In the Gévaudan, for example, a number of servant-girls committed infanticide on children sired by their masters. Everywhere even those who had good relationships with their masters and mistresses regarded them as kind patrons rather than as parents. The analogy with children referred to the relationship of dependence upon and subjugation to the father and mother/master and mistress which both groups shared, not to affective relations.

It is always going to be difficult to distinguish between 'normal' and 'abnormal' behaviour. There does seem to be evidence of the general acceptance of the idea that the interests of the family were uppermost and that relationships had to be ordered to serve them. This does not mean, however, that people lived in accordance with theory. Men, women and children lived together in close proximity and, inevitably, there was friction. Individuals sometimes tried to claim more liberty than was consistent with this theory. There were unhappy, even violent marriages. There was child abuse. There was incest. There was heavy-handed parenting and there were rebellious teenagers. But the solutions proffered in such circumstances were not the dissolution of an unhappy marriage, separation of the child from the parents or the intervention of the state. It was, generally speaking, an appeal to the restoration of harmonious relations by conforming to these norms.

Domestic buildings and family life

We have seen something of the kinds of family structures which you might find in France and the British Isles in the seventeenth century. We are now going to look at some of the material evidence for their lives in their houses and how these can inform us about the structure, economy and relationships of the family. Despite their often spartan appearance, all these houses belonged to better-off people whose way of life reflects common assumptions about the conduct of the household and its communal responsibilities.

You should now turn to Video 10.

Video Exercise 1   Watch Parts 1 and 2 of the video and make notes on what you can learn about the composition of the family and the way in which they used the space in the Maison Cornec.

Discussion   We do not know how many people actually lived in the house at one time, but with an arrangement of this type, it is likely that there were two families in residence. One upstairs and one downstairs. The upper floor is heated and has its own drain. We cannot say anything about the relationship between the two families. There is very little private space, no part of either family has a separate existence from the rest, though sleeping quarters are enclosed.

In the house and its immediate surroundings it is clear that the whole household shared in a range of economic activities. Pigs are separated from the residents, but cows occupy the same space, though in a clearly demarcated area of the house.

This lack of separation between humans and animals seems nowadays to be indicative of a rather backward way of life. But consider the facilities of the house: fireplace, fine joinery, storage spaces, running water, and the designation of space on the ground floor for specific activities. This actually is rather a well-planned and commodious house and its size indicates that it was built for someone pretty wealthy. Note the date, 1702. This is not a medieval house, it is a modern house and the money to build it probably came from the local linen trade rather than from agriculture alone.

Video Exercise 2   Now watch Part 3 of the video and make notes on the kinds of family relationships implied in each house.

Discussion   Despite the great difference in size and in facilities, both houses have an important feature in common which is that the main living space is a communal one. Servants and householders live together in a public space, an essentially medieval arrangement. Washington differs from Woodhouses in that cooking takes place in a different space and there is, therefore, some separation between servants and employers, but there is no separate *living* space for servants. We have seen how servants were to be regarded as part of the household. Living arrangements such as these show how this occurred.

But in both houses, again, it is clear that there could not have been large numbers of distantly related people. Such households could not have contained, for example, grandparents and two or three complete families of married sons and daughters.

Examining prescriptive literature

Above (pp.130–2) we discussed the issue of conforming to norms in order to restore harmonious relations within households. An examination of printed and manuscript prescriptive literature might help us to understand these norms. We should, however, always be aware that these writings did not, for the most part, have the status of law. When we read a work such as William Gouge's *Of Domesticall Duties* we have to prepare ourselves by

1   establishing who the author was;

2   what his/her purpose was in writing;

3   what audience was envisaged.

(If you studied the Arts Foundation course you will find this approach familiar.) Then we need to be on our guard for we must not assume that the work was widely read, let alone obeyed. Imagine, for example, that the specific work has the same status as Dr Benjamin Spock's childcare manual in the 1960s. How many people read it? How many people slavishly obeyed its advice? Were there no opposing manuals?

There were many different categories of prescriptive writing on the family in England and Scotland. There was the Bible itself. There was sermon literature which interpreted the scriptural message for contemporary congregations. There were devotional works. There were Conduct Books. There were contributions to on-going debates about nature of human relationships and roles. Apart from the first two categories, these works were written by an élite for an élite – the literate middling sort of people. We should not assume though that all sermon literature, for example, had the same audience or the same concern to define and praise family relationships. Protestants and Catholics spoke from a different perspective. Richard Baxter, of whom you have read in Unit 7, in 1656 was eager to cultivate household worship for:

> what are we like to do ourselves to the reforming of a congregation, if all the work be cast on us alone, and masters of families neglect the necessary duty of their own. If any good be begun by the ministry in any soul, a careless, prayerless, worldly family is likely to stifle it. (Richard Baxter, *Gildas Salvianus or The Reformed Pastor,* 1656; cited in Brown, 1829, pp.158–9)

The English sects of the seventeenth century had distinctive approaches. James Naylor, the Quaker, boasted in his writings of casting off family ties in order to follow God.

One feature of much of the literature is the concern displayed to explore a variety of relationships within the family/household (narrowly defined by twentieth-century historians and demographers as the co-resident nuclear family plus live-in servants) and not simply that between husband and wife. The family was a network of relationships; so was the household. There was a longstanding tradition in England and Scotland of sermons, conduct books and devotional works which saw the essential division in the household as that between the 'governors' (husband and wife together) and 'those that be ruled' (children and servants). This said, the relation between a father and a son was different in many ways from that between the master and the servant. At the same time little, if anything, was said in these works about relations between siblings or between siblings and servants or between children and step-parents or step-siblings. We can speculate why these relations were neglected.

The common ground in all these English and Scottish Protestant writings was provided by reference to the scriptural models but there was room for considerable difference in interpretation and emphasis. What was the approach in the French literature?

Exercise   Read *Anthology*, II.33 and try to see what conclusions they point to about the attitude of French Catholic instructors towards marriage and the family.

Discussion   These texts emphasize the nature of marriage as a sacrament (a means to acquiring salvation) administered at the moment of marriage and efficacious when those who receive the sacrament are properly prepared (through church instruction). The prime positive purpose of marriage is procreation. Holy upbringing of the children of the marriage (which, other manuals emphasize, includes proper administration of correction) will earn the parents merit, thus contributing to their salvation. Its obligations also include union of the spouses, who must support one another physically, emotionally and morally, notwithstanding adverse circumstances. The negative benefits of marriage are also stressed. It protects the participants against the sin of lust. *Anthology*, II.33(B) urges that the church, through the sacrament of marriage, offers support for the couple in their married life and their family. Should the couple reject this help (by, presumably rejecting church marriage and all that entailed) the union will inevitably be unhappy.

In France, the family and household were far less the subject for discussion than they were in England and Wales. The concept of the family as the moral cell of society, upon whose health the health of the whole society depends, is not to the fore. Marriage and the family are necessary evils rather than the means to grace. There does seem, however, to have been a gradual change in emphasis during the period 1500 to 1800. At the beginning of the period the wife is portrayed almost in the same relation to her husband as a daughter (true patriarchy); by the end she is partner and often perceived as a restraining moral force within the home.

A good deal of contemporary English literature dealt with female roles in family and wider society. A modern scholar has categorized these works into:

1   works celebrating the virtue of the good wife;

2   histories of famous women;

3   satires on the general nature of women;

4   responses to these satires.

Exercise   Into which of the above categories would you place the following text? Why?

To keep him good, his wife must be
obedient, mild her housewifery
within doors she must tend; her charge
is that at home; his that at large;
she must be careful; idle wives
vice works on, and to some ill drives:
not toying, fond, nor yet unkind,

not of a weak, dejected mind,
nor yet insensible of loss,
Which doth with care her husband cross:
Nor jealous, but deserving well,
Not gadding, news to know, or to tell;
Her conversation with the best,
In Husband's heart her thought must rest;
thus if she choose, thus use her mate,
He promiseth her happy state.

(Preface to Patrick Hannay, *The Happy Husband,* 1622; cited in Saintsbury, 1905, p.679)

Discussion   Although written in verse form, this text fits in category (1). It describes how (in the author's view) the good wife should behave in relation to her husband. Read in the light of preconceptions about patriarchy, the poem seems to suggest that a wife, if she abides by the rules, will be treated well by her husband.

Patriarchy has become a contentious issue among modern scholars. In a strict sense there was not true patriarchy in either England and Wales or France – that is the authority of the father, while predominant within the nuclear family, was not absolute. For instance, in England and Wales the church insisted that both parties to a marriage must give their free consent to the union, no matter what the view of the parents. When, on marriage, a new household was set up the father of neither spouse retained authority over his offspring. The father of the bride handed over his daughter to the groom; the husband replaced the father. In those French households (and the rather fewer English and Welsh households) where one of the children continued to live with his parents after marriage, this chain of authority was more complicated.

However, the ideal subscribed to was one of a nuclear family defined by co-residence in which the husband had authority over both his wife and the children. In England a wife had no legal identity under the common law. She was *feme coverte*: her husband had the use of and administered the property she brought to the marriage (although he could not alienate it without her consent); she could not make a contract; she could not make a will without his permission. Both the ecclesiastical law and the equity law (that practised in Chancery) allowed her more freedom and protection. In France the legal identity of wives and of all children was denied. In some parts of France sons of whatever age were unable to make contracts without their father's permission until they themselves married. Ultimately, in both societies power within the family rested with the husband and father. Patriarchy was a reality.

But recent work on the English situation points to an experience for wives which often softened the harshness of their legal situation and the accepted social norms. The marriage of Adam and Jane Eyre (revealed to us in a journal kept by Adam in the 1640s), for example, was a marriage which certainly knew its ups and downs and yet operated in many ways as a companionate marriage. The couple had a joint social life. When they quarrelled, sometimes seriously, about her property, her immodest attire, his drinking and bowling, it is true that Adam tried to assert his authority by refusing her conjugal rights until she listened to him. But she would not be bullied. On one occasion she locked him out of the house and 'said she would be master of the house for that night'. Eventually, Adam resolved that harmony must be restored and entered a new year resolution (perhaps a contract) whereby she would forbear to bring up old grievances, he would be a good husband to her, she would do anything he asked her to, except sign away her land and he would cease to try to pressure her into land transactions. Such an example as this does not indicate that all husbands were faced with strong and determined wives – but what it does suggest is that the prescribed relationship between husband and wife was mediated by the personalities of the spouses and their individual circumstances. And it reinforces the strong emphasis in seventeenth-century writing upon the necessity for harmony and partnership in marriage. The conduct books, for example, counselled that the partnership in marriage should be so strong and so well ordered that appeals to the ultimate authority of the father should never be necessary.

A study of other types of literature indicates that many writers regarded women as capable of government at home and abroad and as intellectually able.

In England and Wales the idea of tyranny within the family by either sex was deplored. Similarly the view that women because 'subject' were to be 'servile' was widely attacked. Marriage, said contemporaries, was an unequal partnership in which the husband was superior. But his dominion was not so great that he should treat his wife as a servant. The wife had her own authority within the household. She was able and willing to rule. If she was incapable then this was because she had been 'disabled' by male nurture rather than by nature. There were, moreover, mutual obligations which under God must be obeyed. The philosopher, Thomas Hobbes, wrote in his *Leviathan* that in the state of nature, which preceded civil society, it was the mother who had had absolute authority over her children. Male authority over children and servants derived from an implicit contract made when governments were formed. Unfortunately, Hobbes did not expand upon how or why women were supplanted as authority figures in the household. Presumably, however, the actual authority of women within the household was the starting point for his observations concerning the 'natural' authority of women. (For further discussion of Hobbes see Unit 13.) Some other writers criticized the suggestion that the male's authority was unquestionable. All urged that a virtuous husband was also a necessity. The indications are that in France the official view also was that marriage was a partnership.

Criticism of the whole concept of patriarchal authority within the household had implications for the treatment of wider issues of authority within the church and the state.

Sir Robert Filmer

We shall now turn to a particular text, 'In Praise of the Virtuous Wife' by Sir Robert Filmer, which is appropriate to the context we have just been discussing. However, we need to know a little about the author first.

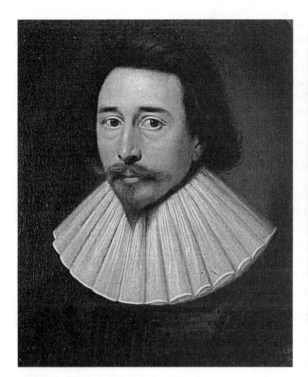

Figure 27
Sir Robert Filmer, *oil on canvas. Private Collection,*
reproduced by courtesy of James Filmer Wilson and Lady
Caroline Ogilvy.

Figure 28
Dame Anne Filmer, *oil on canvas. Private Collection,*
reproduced by courtesy of James Filmer Wilson and Lady
Caroline Ogilvy.

Sir Robert Filmer (*c.*1588–1653) was the eldest of 18 children. He attended Trinity College, Cambridge, left, as was the custom for young gentlemen of the day, without taking a degree, and then moved to Lincoln's Inn in 1604 to study law. It was a cultivated family, whose circle included Ben Jonson and George Herbert, and whose passion was music. Filmer's younger brother Edward was an author who published a collection of French court songs. The family seat housed an important collection of music manuscripts. Robert Filmer was well versed in both classical and contemporary English and continental literature.

He married, in 1618, Anne, daughter of Bishop Martin Heton of Ely. Contrary to popular, and convenient, legend, she was no child bride; she probably married at the peak of her childbearing years. They lived in the Porter's Lodge at Westminster and Anne gave birth there to six of their children, the first five at the close intervals (an average of fourteen months between births) suggestive of her relative youth and perhaps indicating that she did not breastfeed her children. In 1639 the Filmers moved to take up residence at East Sutton Park, Kent, on the death of his father. During the civil war Filmer was a royalist and he spent at least eighteen months imprisoned at Leeds Castle, Kent. While in prison he probably wrote 'In Praise of the Virtuous Wife'. He died in 1653 and the estate passed to his eldest son, Edward, who was then in exile with the English court at Paris.

Exercise   Read now *Anthology*, II.35. Try to get the sense of the document, which is written in somewhat unfamiliar language and in a characteristic form of the period – question and answer. The treatise begins with a text taken from the Book of Proverbs in the Old Testament. The points in the treatise that follows always refer back to and explicate that text.

When you have done that, try to extract the main points of Filmer's argument concerning the fifth commandment.

Discussion   Here are some of the points I would expect you to have noted:

1   Lines 1–8. The fifth commandment – Honour thy father and thy mother – is said to contain three categories of duties or obligations. These are: that between a superior and an inferior; that between equals; that to ourselves.

2   The first category is further considered. There are public relations and obligations between king and subjects; there are private relations and obligations between husband and wife, parents and children, masters and servants. In these relations the doctrine of 'chastisement' must be observed, as also the respect due to age.

3   The second category is further considered. Among equals the doctrine of 'manners' pertains; its opposite is contained in relations governed by 'pride'.

4   The third category is further considered. Our relations towards ourselves must be governed by concern for our good reputation. 'Our owne good fame'.

Exercise   How does Filmer expand upon the role of the wife in the relationship between superiors and inferiors?

Discussion   A multitude of scriptural texts are used to exemplify her character, her relationship with God and her relationship with her husband. The key sentences here are 'These privileges had not been granted if women could not be virtuous. This ought to be their comfort...' (p.139, ll.9–25, p.140).

Exercise   What does Filmer think are the probable objections to his argument about the wife's role and how does he answer them?

Discussion   I would list the following as the most obvious:

1   Woman was the first sinner. He refutes this on the grounds that Eve provided the occasion and not the cause of Adam's fall and that she did so, not out of malicious intent but out of 'ignorant love'. Moreover, she was punished more than Adam. Finally, Mary was the occasion though not the cause of salvation through Christ (p.140, ll.36–43).

2   Women have been most wicked. Filmer counters that if there have been some very evil women, then there have also been women who were better than men. He gives many examples (p.140, last line to p.141, l.24).

3   A woman is the weaker vessel. Filmer urges that this weakness can
       be a virtue. It permits harmonious relations within the family
       (p.141, ll.25–40).

I shall now take you through the rest of the text highlighting other examples.

Filmer goes on to state that the woman 'is the crown of her husband
or lord' only if she is virtuous 'and marry willingly'. If she marries for lust,
beauty, honour or wealth then 'she is a hellish screechowl not a heavenly
nightingale'. A good woman can protect a man against melancholy and
adultery.

Again there are objections that are refuted.

The crown of gold may be an affliction. True, but 'it is better even
then to marry than to burn with distracting lust' (p.141, l.41–p.142, l.23).

Just as a king may not give or sell his gold crown, neither can a wife
be put away for sickness of mind or body, for false religion, for murder or
other crimes or adultery.

She is a fit ornament when she is virtuous. Filmer explains that a
wife shames her husband if she only does good when her husband com-
mands it; if she refuses to do good even when he does command it or if
she shames him openly when 'she reproveth him before others' rather
than persuading him gently to do good. In the first sense she casts suspicion on her husband for selecting an ungodly wife; in the second she
places her husband in the way of temptation as she defies both God and
himself; in the third sense she casts shame upon him publicly or 'pri-
vately without leave'. Seemingly contrary scriptural examples – those of
Abigail, Eve and Job's wife – are cited and dismissed (p.142, l.24–p.143,
l.34).

He then indicates the two-fold nature of a woman's virtue or wis-
dom. Her Christianity. Her worldly role: for pleasure 'as music'; for her
contribution in domestic management; for the usefulness of her skills in
both private and public life. In public she practices 'physic and surgery',
in private 'curious arts'. Modern readers are left speculating what these
'curious arts' might be! (p.143, ll.35–41).

It is worthwhile noting that this text is absolutely full of interest for
our topic. Here is Robert Filmer an anti-feminist rising up in defence of
the virtuous woman against those who thought women had no potential
for virtue. Not only that, he finds plenty of examples.

Exercise   How is the woman characterized in the opening text and, indeed, in the
passages we have so far examined in some detail?

Discussion   I would expect you to have noted some, if not all, of the following.

1   Woman is seen as a wife and, therefore, only in relation to a hus-
       band.

2   Woman is described as an ornament to her husband, a crown of
       gold.

3   Filmer explains that a woman requires virtue to be an ornament.

4. Filmer shows that some women have fulfilled this role because women have potential for virtue.

5 The word 'ornament' and the concept of the 'crown of gold' suggest something that a man chooses to wear, that is, whatever its advantages, dispensable.

6 Little is said of the relationship of the husband to the wife and his obligations, if any, to enhance her existence.

Exercise Now read p.143, l.35–p.144, l.12. How can women be rendered virtuous wives?

Discussion These bring nobility to women as arms and learning do to men. In this place is only meant housewifery which must be attained, and kept attained by three means. 1. If they be broken of their will when they are young. (That is, disciplined to become 'good wives'). 2. If they be kept in service far from home. 3. If they be not married until they be skilful in housewifery.

These lines refer to the role of the parents in training their daughters up to be housewives, using appropriate disciplines; to the apparently widespread custom of placing adolescents in service in the homes of kith, kin and acquaintances to acquire further training in housewifery; to the need to delay marriage until a young woman had acquired given skills that would include practical and managerial aspects of housewifery.

Exercise In lines 2–12 (p.144) ·Filmer goes on to say something yet more intriguing. What do you think these lines mean?

Discussion A woman's capacity to become a virtuous wife depends in part upon (a) the qualities of her husband who must not squander their money or interfere with her management of the household (b) not having another woman with 'authority' in the household (that is, an interfering mother or mother-in-law countermanding her orders); and (c) the presence of well-trained servants attuned to her methods.

We shall now continue to work through the rest of the text. Filmer points out the consequences of the lack of such virtue in a wife and offers guidance on how to ensure that a wife possesses such virtues (p.144, ll.24–40). He considers the criteria for *choosing* a wife and then, after marriage, *using* her. The prospective husband must look at her mind – she must share his language and religion. I think this means not so much that she must speak English but that they must be – in modern parlance – on the same wave-length. She must not exhibit the sins of pride, lust and covetousness. He must look at her body – if she looks as if she has a contagious disease that might result in separation he should not marry her. Their worldly estates should be equivalent – involving neither marrying significantly above or below his station. Once they are married, she should not be subjected to inappropriate discipline but accorded 'moderate' liberty; she should be mistress of her own household; she should not be entrusted with knowledge beyond her capacity; she should be treated with respect before children, servants and strangers.

Later in the treatise (pp.146–8) Filmer explains in what this liberty consists. He must trust her to be chaste, to govern daughters, maidservants and young sons, and to manage their finances if she seems capable.

Exercise   How will the wife earn this trust?

Discussion   Filmer speaks in terms of negatives: she must be 'void' of ignorance in housewifery, of idleness, of 'bellycheer' [gluttony and love of entertaining at home and abroad], of lust, of vanity in dress and building. 'Of all these caterpillars the most dangerous are idleness and bellycheer!!' Filmer explains in more detail what vices are included in these two 'caterpillars'.

Exercise   How does the wife exhibit her good works? Filmer answers this in terms of her faithfulness and her providence. Look at pp.147–9 and see if you can work out what he meant by these.

Discussion   Her faithfulness seems to consist of her giving her loyalty entirely to her husband and of repaying him always with goodness. She may 'teach him religion'; she may give him affection and solace in time of grief or fear. This faithfulness is not a temporary thing, it will last throughout her life.

Her providence will show itself in three ways – in getting: keeping her house well and cheerfully, entailing hard work producing cloth and food etc., sometimes in retailing, in organizing the day; in employment: seeming to encompass the administration of their common property – for example, in charitable giving at home and abroad; in attiring the family and the household; and in selling goods; and in preserving or keeping: the spiritual guidance and witness that she offers all her family and her management of the household ensuring that all is well done and that neither commodities nor time be wasted or spent purposelessly.

It is a mistake to think that the text itself contains all that we need to understand it. Analysis of the text is intriguing but the historian profits most by bringing other information to bear upon the text and, also, by seeing the text in relation to other information we possess about family life in the seventeenth century. At the same time we do have to remain sufficiently open to be able to appreciate 'new' features revealed by the text.

At the time when Filmer probably wrote this treatise his own wife, Anne, was bravely and resourcefully managing the family estates and fending off attacks from parliamentary troops.

Exercise Look back through the text and your notes. What indicators are there that Filmer wrote this treatise during the civil war?

Discussion There are many references to warfare, sieges and warlike women in the treatise. Courage is singled out as a feminine characteristic, as is independence.

We may infer that personal experience of his wife's resourceful and courageous management of their own household during these years informed his appreciation of the virtuous wife in this text.

 Filmer has been identified as the only royalist political theorist who asserted an extension of royal power as opposed to a defence of the power the monarch already possessed on the grounds that within the household the father's power was absolute and that the analogy between the father and the king was a perfect one. Filmer was penning these thoughts in *Patriarcha* at approximately the same time as 'In Praise of the Virtuous Wife'. Filmer wrote three essays specifically treating aspects of family government and a number of theological pieces. These essays should be read alongside *Patriarcha* (1643) if we are to understand Filmer's position on family and state relations. Two of them – 'In Praise of the Virtuous Wife' and 'Touching Marriage and Adultery' – are of special interest. While they do not contradict his view of the sovereignty of the father in the household and the king in the state, they represent a reasoned argument for a real partnership between husband and wife which allows power and authority to wives in time of emergency and in specific circumstances. For further discussion of *Patriarcha* see Unit 13.

Filmer's arguments had in mind a household which was structured around a unit of parents and their children, where the lines of authority were relatively simple. As a model, therefore, it was seemingly more appropriate for English, Welsh, lowland Scottish, English-settled Irish and northern French society than for southern France, Highland Scotland and Ireland outside the Pale.

The treatise, which was designed for manuscript circulation, was far from unconventional, however, and it should be studied in the context of an extensive genre of literature exploring the role and attributes of the good wife. In such works relations within the co-resident family (the household) are modelled upon a scriptural patriarchal family. In practice marriage in early modern times was a partnership albeit an unequal one. The husband was the ultimate authority. Expectations were placed upon both spouses to perform particular functions. Historians have often looked back and described a differentiation of role in terms of public and private – the husband performing on the public stage and the wife on the domestic. But Filmer's treatise indicates that this is too simplistic a view.

Had you known that Filmer was associated with a highly patriarchal view of the governance of family and state, how do you think this would have influenced your reading of this text?

Conclusion

There clearly was a relationship between the ideal and the actual forms of the household and the authority relations within it. Describing these relations as patriarchal may, however, be misleading if we assume that in a patriarchal household the father/husband is all powerful and the dependent members (wife and children and servants) totally powerless. Moreover the nature of the patriarchal household in southern France was often very different and much more complex than that in England, Wales, northern France and lowland Scotland.

Granted this similarity between the descriptive and the prescriptive family in many parts of the British Isles and France, it is more difficult to decide whether the state and the church influenced the form of the household and power relations within the household more than did economic or other factors. Moreover, an examination of the available evidence suggests that the power and authority of the male head of household was often much less than the governors of church and state hoped.

I do not, for one moment, wish to suggest that within the household there was egalitarianism or even the hope of equality. Demonstrably there was not. But we are missing the point if we imply that equality was even at issue. Contemporaries were conditioned to accept that the household must function according to scriptural precepts. The scriptural model accorded co-residents specific roles and relationships. Individuals often found it difficult to bow to the practical implications of these and often perceived that other household members were overstepping the bounds of the scriptural teaching but they rarely if ever articulated a demand for equality. Harmony and not rebellion within the family was what was strived for if not achieved. Grasping this is often made more difficult by the fact that the examples we have of family relations *are* frequently taken from what we might call conflict situations – legal battles over inheritance or ownership, divorce and separation suits, correspondence regarding unpopular marriages or problems in everyday life – or are attempts to smooth relations.

Understanding something more of prescriptive and descriptive domestic relations might help us to understand more fully the political theory of the time that so often employed a domestic analogy. It should also prevent us too blindly assuming a great and uniform divide in domestic relations between the past and the present. The accurate description of household relations in the early modern period is no simple matter.

References

Brown, W. (1829), *The Reformed Pastor*, Glasgow.

Chaytor, M. (1980), 'Household and kinship: Ryton in the late sixteenth and early seventeenth centuries', *History Workshop Journal*, 10.

Gouge, W. (1622), *Of Domesticall Duties*, Epistle, sig.2v.

Laslett, P. (1983), *The World We Have Lost Further Explored*, Methuen, London.

Laslett, P. and Wall, R., (eds) (1972), *Household and Family in Past Time*, Cambridge University Press, Cambridge.

Mendelson, S.H. (1985), 'Stuart women's diaries and occasional memoirs', in M. Prior (ed.), *Women in English Society, 1500–1800*, Methuen, London.

Molé, M. (1855–7), *Mémoires*, vol.II, edited by A. Champollion-Figeac, Société de l'Histoire de France, 4 vols, Paris.

Pillorget, R. (1991), *La Tige et le Rameau: Familles anglaises et françaises xvie – xviiie siècle*, Calmann-Levy, Paris.

Saintsbury, G. (ed.) (1905), *Minor Poets of the Caroline Period*, 3 vols, Clarendon Press, Oxford.

Index